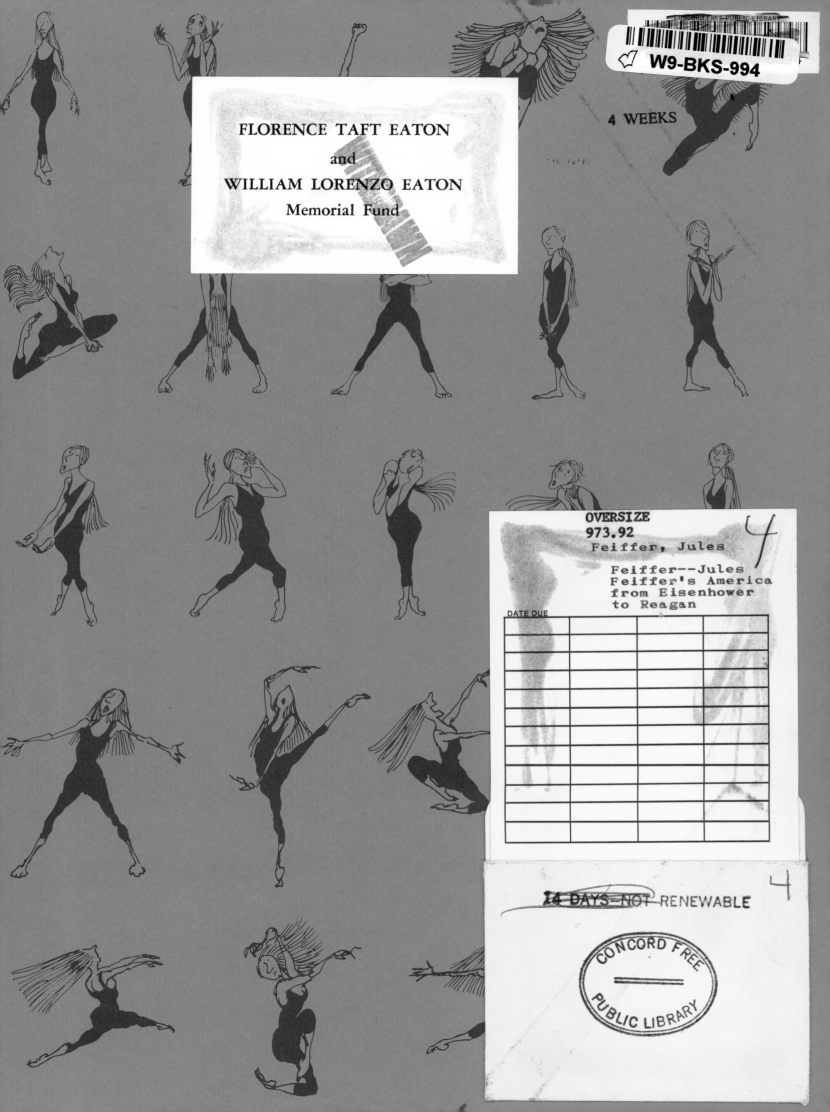

ALSO BY JULES FEIFFER

JULES FEIFFER'S AMERICA
FROM EISENHOWER TO REAGAN
EDITED BY STEVEN HELLER

Alfred A. Knopf · New York · 1982

THIS IS A BORZOI BOOK
PUBLISHED BY ALFRED A. KNOPF, INC.

Library of Congress Cataloging in Publication Data
Feiffer, Jules.
    Feiffer—Jules Feiffer's America from Eisenhower to Reagan.

    "A Borzoi book."
    1. United States—Politics and government—1945-   —
Caricatures and cartoons. 2. United States—Civilization—1945-   —
Caricatures and cartoons. 3. American wit and humor, Pictorial. I.
Heller, Steven. II. Title. III. Title: America from Eisenhower
to Reagan.
E839.5.F44 1982   973.92   82-47815
ISBN 0-394-52846-8   AACR2
ISBN 0-394-71279-X (pbk.)

Manufactured in the United States of America
First Edition

FOR
KATE FEIFFER

INTRODUCTION

I am nervous about this book. On the one hand, I don't mind a little self-celebration. On the other, retrospectives make me uneasy; they smell of entombment. I like to think that the work I do next year will be better than this year's and better than anything in this book.

Still, I like this work. I can read it over and still get something out of it. But there is a lot of talent out there today. I admire and envy some of it. I worry about keeping up. I worry about my place in the pack. I worry about whether I'm radical enough anymore, meaning that I'm probably not; and, if not, how I should go about upgrading my radicalism. The one thing I don't want, as I advance through my middle years, is to mellow. I'm 53.

The cartoons in this volume go from 1956 to 1982. This was intended as a twenty-fifth anniversary salute to myself, but I kept putting it off. If Steven Heller had not volunteered to piece it together, nothing would have been done. Steve edited the book and I edited his editing. So I surrendered responsibility, maintained authority and felt objective.

In October of 1956, after failing to sell cartoons to more conventional markets, I began giving them for free to *The Village Voice*, a struggling Greenwich Village weekly published and gently edited by Ed Fancher and Dan Wolfe. The cartoon was in strip form and I called it *Sick, Sick, Sick*. It was designed as a weekly satiric comment on the people I knew, the young urban middle class, their work habits, sex urges and family antagonisms. You must remember that this was in another time. Sex was treated as either dirty or discreet, not right as material for humor in family newspapers or on TV.

Sociologists referred to contemporary college students as "the silent generation," to my own age group as "conformists," to my elders as "status seekers" or "organization men." We were told we were "affluent." One of our most serious problems was "the leisure problem." Another problem was "alienation." Also "anxiety." Not to overlook "apathy." Poverty was not one of our problems. We were told that poverty ended with the war and the post-war boom. Negroes were known to have problems. We were sympathetic, despised the South, would have lynched it were we not liberals. We were against capital punishment and in favor of civil liberties for those falsely accused of being communists, and against civil liberties for those correctly accused.

We believed in leadership, didn't think presidents or their aides lied. Congressmen lied, but that was part of a great tradition, part of our folklore, a subject of humor. You could joke about corrupt Congressmen. You couldn't joke about corrupt presidents or corrupt churchmen or J. Edgar Hoover. It was in bad taste.

We believed in education. We believed in science.

4.

5.

6.

We believed in experts and qualified sources. We believed we were good and the Russians were bad and we were better dead than Red. Everything was in place.

I did not mean for the cartoon to go into politics. I was more interested in satirizing my own kind: Greenwich Village make-out men, wine and cheese parties, modern dancers, girls who were too busy to see you because they were washing their hair, bosses who thought it was a violation of friendship to ask for a raise, anxious fathers and possessive mothers, Village men and women explaining themselves in an endless babble of self-interest, self-loathing, self-searching and evasion. My aim was to take the Robert Benchley hero and launch him into the Age of Freud.

Bernard Mergendeiler was my victim-hero and not hard to come by: I composed him out of my own life and the lives of friends. It was taken for granted in Bernard's world that men slept with women, or hoped to. Except for fans of Peter Arno, this piece of information was unknown to most readers of cartoons in family magazines and newspapers. People who slept with each other were shunted off to *Playboy, Esquire* and the girlie magazines where they displayed themselves in panties and boxer shorts and spoke in off-color one-liners. Sex was isolated from other facts of life. It was in bad taste. Bad taste was bad business in the family media. So that which dominated the waking lives of every unmarried male of my acquaintance was treated as if it did not exist.

Bernard was a young urban liberal given to anxiety attacks, stomachaches and obsessive confessionals. He either had bad sex or no sex; either way he felt guilty. He understood and accepted the fact that all the truly desirable Smith, Vassar and Sarah Lawrence girls he met were sleeping with huge unemployed actors or black men. In the coffeehouses he hung out in, it meant much to him to talk about *meaningful relationships* with girls who weren't *hostile, aggressive* or *castrators*.

The Dancer was Bernard's female counterpart, abused and exploited by men no less than he was by women, but where Bernard grew defensive and angry over the years, the Dancer retained her faith. She danced, fell, got to her feet, tripped, sailed aloft, came crashing to earth, rose stubbornly and kept dancing.

I found out soon enough that these characters, self-obsessed as they were, could not live independently of Dwight D. Eisenhower, the president of their existence. Eisenhower's presidency surrounded me and mine, not in its politics—the wise among us shunned politics—but in a Cold War mood of muted anxiety and isolation that bled out of the White House into offices, bars, coffeehouses and bedrooms. We took Ike to work and to bed. He gave us complacency and a nervous stomach. He

A
DANCE
TO
SPRING.

The first dancer cartoon.

didn't know it, he didn't care one way or the other; it was his time. Among the people I ran into, there was a lot of arrogance and very little self-worth. Those in search of answers read Riesman's *The Lonely Crowd* and, to recover, read Fromm's *The Art of Loving*.

In the first month of *Sick, Sick, Sick*, my drawing style embraced and retreated from the styles of William Steig, Robert Osborn and the UPA animated cartoon studio. I knew what I wanted to write but I didn't know how to present my case. From week to week my style changed so sharply that a casual reader might have thought I was different cartoonists. It took six months for my head and line to agree on an approach.

I was in psychotherapy and took full advantage of it. I scared myself by my anger and my politics. I scared my readers. "How do you get away with it?" I was repeatedly asked. No one was used to getting away with

anything anymore. No one marched. Few protested. Only those who didn't mind risking their futures signed petitions. My readers and I became conspirators.

And it was in a spirit of conspiracy that I slunk down to the Village Vanguard to see Mort Sahl or Mike Nichols and Elaine May. Or skulked off to Chicago to see Second City. We were members of a comic underground, meeting in cabarets and cellar clubs, making startlingly grave and innovative jokes about virginity, Jewish mothers, HUAC and J. Edgar Hoover.

Time and *Newsweek* labeled what we did as sick humor. I replied that it was not sick humor, but that society was sick, you understand? and that I was commenting on a sick society, you know what I mean? and that I hated sick jokes, you get it? I turned blue explaining myself. Eventually, it was simpler to drop the title *Sick, Sick, Sick* and rename the cartoon *Feiffer*.

In 1958, my first collection of cartoons was published, on the basis of which Hugh Hefner offered me $500 a month to draw for *Playboy*. Since the *Voice* still did not pay contributors, it was the first regular money I made doing the work I cared about. My attitude was often non-*Playboy* or anti-*Playboy*. Rather than object, Hefner suggested ways of making my points stronger. In addition to his better-known qualities, he was a wonderful cartoon editor, the best I've had.

In 1960, I was courted by the Hall Syndicate for national syndication. I told them I was worried about selling out. I was afraid of being censored. I was afraid of losing my status as a cult cartoonist.

Newspapers in those days were not in the habit of running opposition voices, not in columns and certainly not in cartoons. After a year of syndication I began to see censorship not as a problem but as a form of affirmation, of quality control. If they didn't run me, it meant I was doing something right. Twenty-two years later I appear in more papers that I ever imagined—that is, considerably fewer than any other famous cartoonist and just enough to break even.

This anthology is laid out for purposes of convenience and coherence, according to presidents, beginning with "The Ike Age" and ending with the age of Reagan or "Movie America." The various cartoons stay within their presidential groupings but, aside from that, chronology is spurned. We tried to put it together to read fast, orderly and good, so I plead with you not to skip around to find favorites or you will make hash of our hard work. Begin here and read straight through. I will make comments along the way.

Jules Feiffer
March 1982

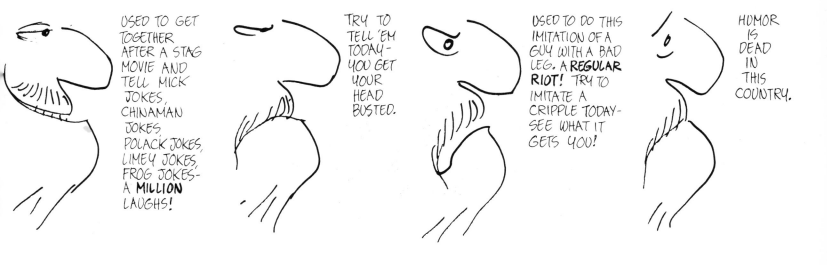

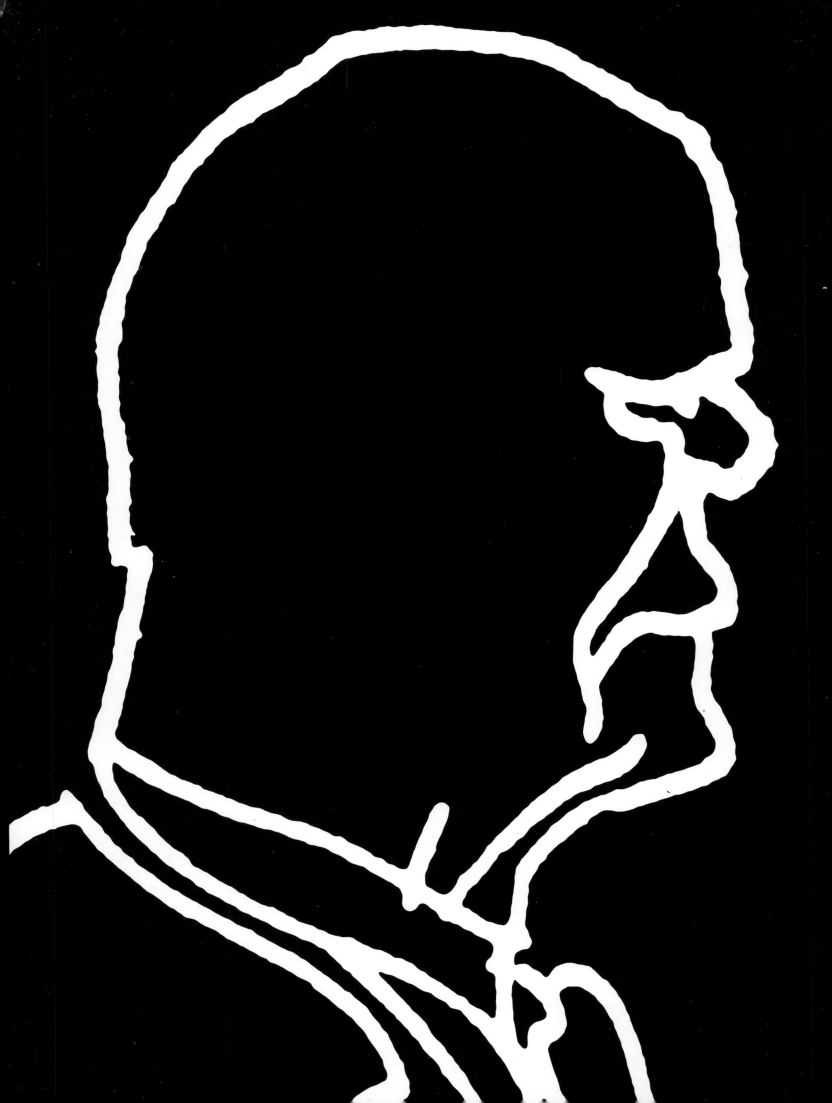

THE IKE AGE

I don't like noticing that the themes I started out with more than two decades ago are back. Nothing gets settled. The Cold War heats up again. Reactionary politics re-emerge. Racism, out of fashion for the shortest of whiles, is now being thoughtfully reconsidered, even by some liberals. A new arms race, new interventions in Latin America, a revitalized CIA, even the long-discounted theory that nuclear war is winnable. That endless list, overly familiar and psychically numbing, as if every twenty years we restage the last generation's debates, few lessons learned, little or no historic memory.

The Bomb was a major fact of life during the '50s, just as now. If young men of my age and class didn't worry about girls and cars and hi-fi's, a fair percentage of us worried or deliberately chose not to worry about the Bomb. The Bomb seemed to symbolize our post-war helplessness. We were the biggest, richest, most powerful country in history and we felt surrounded. The Bomb, *our* creation, in production of which we outnumbered the Russians many times over, was translated through Cold War mystique into their weapon.

Children took shelter under desks during school recesses, called air raid drills, at a time when the Russians had no delivery system other than the imaginations of school principals. The Bomb was a staple, out there as a threat but also a blessing: It made future war unthinkable. That was good. But it made much else in life also hard to think about.

What was the advantage of one American being worth ten Germans or Japs if, when the test came, we all went BOOM? Unthinkable war robbed armed combat of its glory, idealism, romance and overriding religious and spiritual advantages. It took God off our side and made him a neutral. Optimism leaked like classified secrets out of our system. War made us righteous. The absence of war made us self-righteous. War made us brave. The absence of war made us scared. War made us united and brought us out of the Depression. The absence of war made us affluent and brought us self-doubt; depression and war were by comparison a definite spiritual plus.

One can usually tell the true temper of a time by analyzing its popular arts. Movies tell the story. Depression heroes met the Cold War and turned cynical on us. James Cagney, who was a gangster in the '30s because society made him so, became a gangster in the '50s because he was a paranoid schizophrenic. Gary Cooper and James Stewart, our foremost populist folk heroes, became High Noon town marshals and combat pilots, not an illusion left except "them" or "us." That nice boy,

Dick Powell, who sang us through the Depression, changed into a bitter tough guy, while Bogart, the epitome of the breed but with a moral conscience, wound up as the cowardly, miserable Fred C. Dobbs and Captain Queeg.

Innocence went out with the Bomb and McCarthyism. Cold War surliness came in, followed shortly thereafter by Eisenhower. His was the good-guy presence under which our paranoia was soft-soaped. I hardly drew him. I was more interested in the policies of the Administration than in the man himself. When I finally got around to it, I showed him as a calm managerial type. Too lazy in those years to work from photographs, I cast him from the image in my mind: Daddy Warbucks.

Because he was a great war hero, he could get away with a less strident militancy than his predecessor or his successor; no hardliner was going to accuse Ike of being soft on communism. He was the bland patron of our suffocation. With Ike, the economy prospered, the middle class grew, the attention span died. Millions of Americans went to sleep under his gaze. It was no accident. He liked muddledness. He didn't like communication. Communication was where reporters could get the drop on you.

His press conferences were headlong leaps into verbal gridlock. He would begin with, "Now I want to make this perfectly clear." The death of language followed. He used the press conference as a way to obscure. No one ever successfully untangled his views on civil rights, but when it came to items closer to a Republican's heart, say, the Federal budget, he made himself perfectly clear. He skirted moral issues. When he sent Federal troops to Little Rock to integrate the schools, he made sure we all knew that he was not responding to the pros and cons of racism, he was simply enforcing the law of the land. Later, when black students conducted college sit-ins, Ike denounced them as criminals no different, he said, from Pretty Boy Floyd or Baby Face Nelson.

He ministered to our natural excesses, encouraging the CIA to subvert Iran and Guatemala, restraining his generals from attacking Vietnam. He brokered our spy scares, witch hunts and shelter programs, all but seducing us into thinking them reasonable.

Lucky for us, Sputnik came along. Before Sputnik, the consensus was that the Russians developed their science by stealing it from us. We were the first. Had Sputnik gone up before Ethel and Julius Rosenberg went on trial, it is possible that we would have lacked the passion or purpose to execute them. Sputnik threw us for a loop; a spectacle of mortification and humiliation. *They* got into space first. It signaled the need to end

McCarthyism. Good-old-boy, anti-intellectual, conformist anti-communism was replaced by a more highbrow, overachieving anti-communism.

The center of our Cold War theology moved out of the heartland into Harvard, setting the stage for the Kennedy ascendance. Sputnik provided the first politically reliable Cold War reason to support higher education: We needed it to fight the Russians.

The Cold War was turned into an instrument of social reform. The reason for better housing was to fight communism, the reason for collective bargaining was to fight communism, the reason for civil rights was to fight communism.

Science and the humanities flourished. Political protest surfaced for the first time in years over the issue of the Bomb. Outlaw causes, such as civil liberties, looked better. The civil rights of Southern Negroes gained renewed interest.

Sputnik shot down McCarthyism and crippled Eisenhowerism. It ended the '50s; it opened the door for everything that was to tear us apart over the next decade.

The Russians did it.

I **USED** TO BE A REBEL IN MY YOUTH.

THIS CAUSE... **THAT** CAUSE... (CHUCKLE) I BACKED 'EM **ALL**

BUT I LEARNED.

REBELLION IS SIMPLY A **DEVICE** USED BY THE IMMATURE TO **HIDE** FROM HIS OWN PROBLEMS.

SO I LOST INTEREST IN POLITICS.

NOW WHEN I FEEL AROUSED BY A **CIVIL RIGHTS** CASE OR A **PASSPORT** HEARING....

I **REALIZE** IT'S JUST A DEVICE.

I GO TO MY ANALYST AND WE WORK IT OUT.

YOU HAVE NO IDEA HOW MUCH **BETTER** I FEEL THESE DAYS.

SO I'M GOING OUT WITH THIS GIRL FOR THE FIRST TIME AND WE'RE GOING TO THE MOVIES AND, AS USUAL, I'M THROWING OUT MY BREAD CRUMBS.

AND SHE ASKS ME WHAT IS IT THAT I'M DOING AND I TELL HER THAT I'M THROWING OUT BREAD CRUMBS SO I CAN FIND MY WAY HOME BECAUSE I HAVE THIS BAD SENSE OF DIRECTION.

SO SHE LAUGHS LIKE IT'S A BIG JOKE AND I SAY I DON'T SEE WHY MY PERSONAL TROUBLES SHOULD MAKE SUCH A BIG JOKE.

AND THEN SHE SAID "**LOOK**- DON'T WORRY - **I'LL** TAKE YOU HOME!" SO I GOT MAD. I SAID "LOOK- WE EACH HAVE OUR OWN WAY OF FINDING OURSELVES. WHO IS TO SAY **YOURS** IS BETTER THAN **MINE**?"

AND SHE SAYS "YOU CAN'T MAKE A WHOLE LIFE'S PHILOSOPHY OUT OF BREAD CRUMBS." SO RIGHT OUT ON THE STREET WE HAD A FIGHT.

AND I GOT **SO** MAD I WALKED AWAY AND I COMPLETELY FORGOT TO FOLLOW MY BREAD CRUMBS.

AND AN AMAZING THING HAPPENED - I HAD NO TROUBLE GETTING HOME.

IT SEEMS TO MAKE MY WHOLE PAST LIFE INVALID.

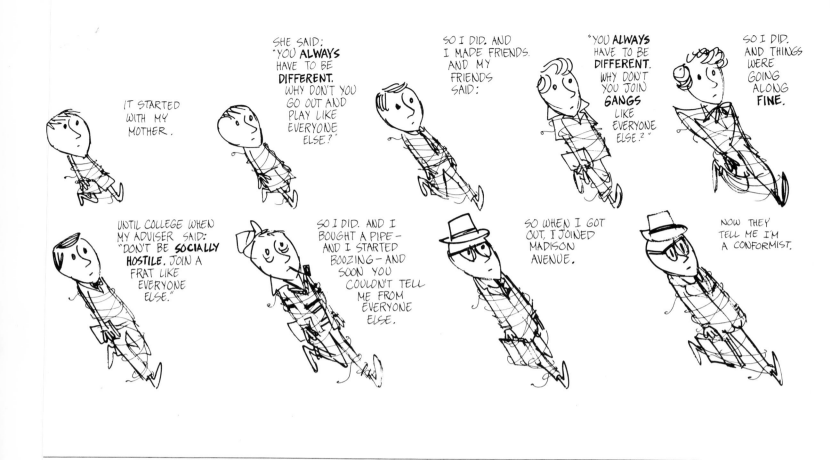

IT STARTED WITH MY MOTHER.

SHE SAID: "YOU **ALWAYS** HAVE TO BE **DIFFERENT**. WHY DON'T YOU GO OUT AND PLAY LIKE EVERYONE ELSE?"

SO I DID. AND I MADE FRIENDS. AND MY FRIENDS SAID:

"YOU **ALWAYS** HAVE TO BE **DIFFERENT**. WHY DON'T YOU JOIN **GANGS** LIKE EVERYONE ELSE?"

SO I DID. AND THINGS WERE GOING ALONG **FINE**.

UNTIL COLLEGE WHEN MY ADVISER SAID: "DON'T BE **SOCIALLY HOSTILE**. JOIN A FRAT LIKE EVERYONE ELSE."

SO I DID. AND I BOUGHT A PIPE— AND I STARTED BOOZING— AND SOON YOU COULDN'T TELL ME FROM EVERYONE ELSE.

SO WHEN I GOT OUT, I JOINED MADISON AVENUE.

NOW THEY TELL ME I'M A CONFORMIST.

ONE DAY HE COMES HOME- HE SAYS -" MAMMA, I AM NOT WELL EMOTIONALLY. I NEED A PSYCHIATRIST."

SO I SEND HIM TO A PSYCHIATRIST. AFTER ALL IF YOU CAN'T HELP YOUR OWN SON, WHAT'S A MOTHER FOR?

SO ONE DAY HE COMES HOME. HE SAYS "MAMMA, PSYCHOANALYSIS HAS TAUGHT ME THAT HOME IS A SMOTHERING INFLUENCE. I'M MOVING OUT."

SO I FIND HIM HIS OWN APARTMENT. AFTER ALL IF YOU CAN'T HELP YOUR OWN SON, WHAT'S A MOTHER FOR?

I GIVE HIM RENT MONEY. I GIVE HIM PSYCHIATRIST MONEY. I GIVE HIM A LITTLE EXTRA SO HE COULD ENJOY HIMSELF. LISTEN— WHAT WOULD **I** DO WITH IT? WHAT'S A MOTHER FOR?

SO ONE DAY HE CALLS UP. HE SAYS- "MAMMA, YOU ARE GIVING ME ALL THIS MONEY JUST SO I SHOULD FEEL **GUILTY**! GUILT IS A MOTHER'S WEAPON.

ALL RIGHT, WHY ARGUE? WHAT DOES IT GET YOU? SO I STOP PAYING HIS PSYCHIATRIST AND I STOP PAYING HIS RENT AND I STOP GIVING HIM ANYTHING EXTRA.

SO NOW ITS OVER A MONTH - HE'S DISPOSSESSED, HE CAN'T FIND A JOB. HIS PSYCHIATRIST IS SU'ING HIM.

BUT LISTEN- SO LONG AS HE'S HAPPY.

NOW LET ME MAKE MYSELF CLEAR.

NOW WE HAVE A LAW AND WE ARE A COUNTRY GOVERNED BY LAW. I WANT YOU TO KNOW I FEEL **STRONGLY** ABOUT THAT.

NOW THERE ARE LAWS WE LIKE AND LAWS WE DON'T LIKE. BUT— AND I WANT TO MAKE THIS CLEAR— WE MUST **OBEY** OUR LAWS OR ELSE WE COULD AID COMMUNISM.

NOW HERE IS THE **LAW OF THE LAND.** AND THAT IS THAT AND WE MUST ENFORCE IT.

NOW THE REST OF THE WORLD IS WATCHING— LET ME MAKE THAT CLEAR— AND WHETHER WE LIKE IT OR NOT— LOTS OF THEM ARE **COLORED**.

BUT THAT'S **NATURE'S** LAW AND WE MUST LIVE WITH IT. I CAN'T STRESS THAT TOO FIRMLY.

NOW LET'S PULL TOGETHER **VOLUNTARILY** AND THAT WILL SOLVE IT ALL AND WHETHER WE LIKE IT OR NOT- FORGE AHEAD.

AND THE REST OF THE WORLD WILL RESPECT US FOR OUR MORAL STAND.

I DON'T GET AROUSED ANYMORE.

NOR DO I NOR DO I.

SAY SOMETHING TO AROUSE ME.

MISSILE MADNESS!

MISSILE MADNESS. YES, THAT'S A GOOD ONE. THAT CERTAINLY SHOULD HAVE AROUSED ME. BUT NO IT DOESN'T.

ATOMIC HOLOCAUST!

AH, THAT USED TO BE A VERY EFFECTIVE ONE. YEARS AGO I GOT AROUSED ALL THE TIME ON ATOMIC HOLOCAUST. BUT NOW—

BRINKS-MANSHIP! GUNBOAT DIPLOMACY! QUEMOY! MATSU!

VERY GOOD. VERY GOOD. FOR A MOMENT THERE I ALMOST FELT AROUSED. I GUESS ITS BECAUSE THEY'RE SO CURRENT.

DO YOU THINK WE'VE TURNED APATHETIC?

APATHY IS SUCH A **BAD** WORD. I'D HATE TO THINK ITS APATHY WE SUFFER FROM.

LETS JUST CALL IT FAITH.

SO ONCE THERE WERE FIVE MILLION PEOPLE UNEMPLOYED.

YOU'RE KIDDING

SO SOME PEOPLE SAID "LETS START A PUBLIC HOUSING PROGRAM" BUT THAT COULD MEAN GOVERNMENT INTERFERENCE SO SOME PEOPLE COMPLAINED— SO ANYHOUSE THEY DIDN'T DO IT.

GOLLY

SO THEN SOME PEOPLE SAID "LETS BUILD NEW SCHOOLS" BUT THAT COULD MEAN GOVERNMENT INTERFERENCE SO SOME PEOPLE COMPLAINED— SO ANYHOW THEY DIDN'T DO IT.

GOLLY

SO THEN THERE WAS THIS PLANE AND ONE DAY BY ACCIDENT IT LET GO A **BIG BOMB**.

DID IT GO **BAROOM?**

NO - IT WENT—

BAGADARAZAP!

BOY- THIS IS GETTING GOOD.

SO IT LEFT A GIANT BIG HOLE SO THEY HAD TO HIRE A LOT OF PEOPLE TO FILL IT. SO THAT GAVE THEM AN IDEA.

WHAT? WHAT? WHAT?

THEY STARTED AN **ACCIDENTAL BOMB DROPPING** PROGRAM.

GREAT

AND SOON **EVERYBODY** WAS WORKING!

HOT DOG!

SO THEY ALL LIVED HAPPILY EVER AFTER.

YOU MEAN SOME PEOPLE DIDN'T COMPLAIN?

NOBODY COMPLAINS ABOUT NATIONAL DEFENSE, DOPEY.

I HAD A DREAM THE OTHER NIGHT THAT THE RUSSIANS ISSUED US AN ULTIMATUM. EITHER WE SURRENDER TO THEM OR FACE DESTRUCTION FROM THEIR ULTIMATE WEAPON.  — NO KIDDING.

WE TURN IT DOWN AND WAIT TENSELY TO SEE WHAT HAPPENS. SUDDENLY THE RUSSIANS ANNOUNCE THEY ARE WITHDRAWING ALL THEIR TROOPS FROM EASTERN EUROPE.  I CAN'T **BELIEVE** IT.

"IT'S A **TRICK**" EVERYBODY HERE CRIES. WE DOUBLE OUR DEFENSE BUDGET.  WHAT **ELSE**?

THEN THE RUSSIANS ANNOUNCE THEY ARE DISBANDING THEIR — **WHOLE** ARMY. "THEY'RE TRYING TO LULL US INTO FALSE SECURITY," OUR EXPERTS SCREAM. WE **TRIPLE** OUR DEFENSE BUDGET.  **WHO** WOULDN'T?

THE NEXT DAY RUSSIA AGREES TO ALL WESTERN TERMS ON DISARMAMENT INSPECTION. WE IMMEDIATELY **TOUGHEN** OUR TERMS AND RESUME NUCLEAR TESTING. A DAY LATER THE RUSSIANS ANNOUNCE THEY'RE **DISMANTLING** ALL THEIR MISSILES.  GOOD **HEAVENS!**

WELL, YOU HAVE NEVER **SEEN** SUCH HELL BREAK LOOSE. THE DEMOCRATS — CHARGE THAT RUSSIA CAN ONLY AFFORD TO DIS-MANTLE BECAUSE OF THE ADMINIS-TRATION'S FAILURE TO CLOSE THE **MISSILE** GAP. FIST FIGHTS BREAK OUT IN CONGRESS.  OUR CON-GRESS?

THEN THE RUSSIANS SEND US THE NAMES OF **ALL** THEIR SPIES — AND HAVE THEM TURN THEMSELVES IN. "IF THEIR OWN **SPIES** CAN'T TRUST THEM, CAN **WE**?" ASK THE NEWSPAPERS.  GOOD POINT. VERY GOOD POINT.

PANIC RAGES. LONDON AND BONN GET INTO A FIGHT OVER THE **SMALL CAR** MARKET. PARIS SIDES WITH BONN AND — SENDS TROOPS TO PROTECT THE ENGLISH CHANNEL.  **MY** PARIS?

THE MIDDLE EAST GOES TO WAR. THE ORG-ANIZATION OF — AMERICAN STATES INVADES CUBA FOR VIO-LATING THE MONROE DOCTRINE. FRANCE QUITS N.A.T.O. AND MISSILE STOCKS FALL IN THE U.S. — THE PRESIDENT ADOPTS A WAIT AND SEE ATTITUDE.  MY PARIS.

THERE ARE **BANK** RIOTS IN THE STREETS OF NEW YORK. CIVIL DEFENSE IS IN AN **UPROAR**. DR. TELLER WARNS THAT OUR LAST CHANCE IS TO DIG A BIG HOLE AND HIDE IN IT. GOVERNOR ROCKEFELLER IS FOR **SMALLER** HOLES PAID FOR BY A CIGARETTE TAX.  WHAT A **SHAME** — HE'S WITH-DRAWN.

WITHIN A MONTH THE WEST HAS FALLEN APART. RUSSIA IS ALL SET TO RE-ARM AND MARCH— WHEN ITS INVADED BY RED CHINA. THATS WHEN I WOKE UP.  **WHAT** A DREAM!

 ITS A GOOD THING WE HAVE PEOPLE IN POWER WHO CAN HANDLE THE SITUATION.

NOW I WANT TO MAKE THIS CLEAR. WHEN THE LEADER OF A NATION - A NATION WE HAVE - YOU HAVE UNFRIENDLY RELATIONS, A COLD WAR WITH, WHEN I AS THE HEAD OF ONE THESE SAID NATIONS INVITES AS THE HEAD OF THAT NATION THE HEAD OF THE OTHER NATION OVER HERE FOR A VISIT - IT, AS YOU MAY WELL KNOW, PRESENTS CERTAIN PROBLEMS.

NOW WE HAVE OUR ALLIES AND THEY MUST BE CONSULTED AND THAT OF COURSE IS WHY I AM GOING OVER TO VISIT THEM BEFORE HE COMES TO VISIT US. AT THE SAME TIME WHILE I AM VISITING THEM THEY MUST, OUR EUROPEAN ALLIES, DECIDE FOR THEMSELVES THAT WE, IN HIS VISIT HERE, WILL MAKE NO BILATERAL - NO SWEEPING DECISIONS.

THAT WOULD BE TAKEN - NOT BE TAKEN - WITHOUT PRIOR CONSULTATION ON THE PART OF THOSE COUNTRIES ON WHICH WE MAKE SWEEPING DECISIONS. THIS WILL CALL FOR VISITS BETWEEN THE HEADS OF THESE COUNTRIES BEFORE MY VISIT TO THEM PRIOR TO **HIS** VISIT TO US HERE.

NOW WE DON'T WANT OUR ASIAN ALLIES TO FEEL THAT THESE VISITS, WHICH MAY OR POSSIBLY NOT AFFECT THEM, OR IT MAY NEVER EVEN BE BROUGHT UP - I DON'T AS KNOW YET - TO FEEL LEFT OUT SO EITHER BEFORE I VISIT EUROPE OR VICE VERSA WE WILL SOMETIME IN BETWEEN HIS VISIT TO US ARRANGE TO VISIT, PERHAPS IN HAWAII, OUR ASIAN ALLIES AFTER OF COURSE THEY HAVE CONSULTED WITH INDIA BEFORE OR SOMETIME THE EUROPEAN MEETINGS.

NOT TO IGNORE THE INTERESTS OF OUR LATIN AMERICAN NEIGHBORS TO THE SOUTH OF US WHO, BEFORE I VISIT THERE, AFTER **HIS** VISIT HERE I WILL IN BETWEEN FIND TIME TO VISIT THEM THERE AND SEEK OUT ANY PERTINENT REACTION THAT THEY MIGHT HAVE AND THUS FINALIZE OUR UNITY SO WHEN THE TWO OF US MEET WE WILL HAVE MUCH TO TALK ABOUT.

LET US NOT, HOWEVER, EXPECT ANY EASY SOLUTION.

SO I WAS SITTING IN THE DARK FEELING VERY RESPONSIBLE BECAUSE WHEN THE SIRENS SOUNDED **I** OBEYED THE LAW AND TOOK SHELTER—

WHEN I REALIZED THAT WE HAD BEEN THERE FOR AN **AWFULLY** LONG TIME. AND SOME OF THE OTHERS WERE BEGINNING TO GROW **RESTLESS.** "THE ALL CLEAR **CERTAINLY** SHOULD HAVE SOUNDED BY NOW." SOME PEOPLE SAID.

SO WE FIGURED OUT THE TIME AND IT HAD BEEN OVER FOUR HOURS. SOME OF THE CROWD WANTED TO GO OUT ON THE STREET BUT I'VE ALWAYS BEEN A NATURAL LEADER SO I TOOK CHARGE AND SAID—

"WE TOOK SHELTER BECAUSE THE **LAW** TOLD US TO. IF WE LEAVE OUR SHELTER BEFORE THE **LAW** TELLS US TO, WE'RE AS BAD AS THOSE PEOPLE SITTING OUT IN THE PARK WHO INSIST THIS WHOLE BUSINESS IS INSANE."

EVERYONE AGREED THAT WE CERTAINLY WANTED TO STAY WITHIN THE **LAW.** CALM WAS RESTORED. AFTER TWO MORE HOURS WENT BY A NERVOUS MOTHER SAID—"LISTEN, I'M SURE I HEAR **SOME** MOVEMENT OUT THERE! MAYBE THE SIREN HAS BROKEN."

"**YES,**" CRIED EVERYONE. "THE SIREN **MUST** HAVE BROKEN!" BUT **ONCE** MORE I BROUGHT LOGIC TO THE SCENE.

I SAID, "THE **LAW** SAYS WE **MUST** WAIT FOR THE SIREN. IF WE LEAVE **BEFORE** WE HEAR THE SIREN EVEN IF IT **IS** BROKEN WE'RE AS BAD AS THOSE PEOPLE SITTING OUT IN THE PARK WHO INSIST THIS WHOLE BUS-INESS IS INSANE."

EVERYONE AGREED OF COURSE. WE BEGAN SINGING HYMNS AND RECOUNTING CHILD-HOOD EXPERIENCES OF BEING LOCKED IN CLOSETS.

AFTER THE TENTH HOUR THE GROUP WANTED TO SELECT SOMEONE WHO DIDN'T **MIND** BREAKING THE LAW TO GO OUT AND FORAGE FOR FOOD.

SO ONCE **MORE** I HAD TO USE LOGIC. I SIMPLY POINTED OUT THAT SUCH AN ACT WOULD MAKE US **ALL** CONSPIRATORS AND THEREFORE AS **LAW**-DEFIANT AS THOSE PEOPLE SIT-TING OUT IN THE PARK WHO INSIST THIS WHOLE BUSINESS IS INSANE.

IT'S BEEN THREE DAYS NOW AND THOSE WHO ARE STILL CONSCIOUS ARE BEGIN-NING TO STIR. PRETTY SOON I'LL HAVE TO SPEAK UP AGAIN.

WITHOUT PROPER RESPECT FOR THE LAW SOCIETY MUST CRUMBLE.

Boom

Once...

the surface of the earth looked like this...

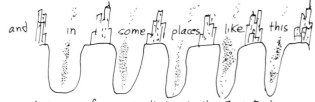

and in some places, like this

and it was, of course, all due to the Bomb tests.

Almost every country had its own Bomb.

If you've got a Bomb you're supposed to test it.

Like to see if it works.

After each explosion the test areas were filled by government scientists who took readings and checked their instruments and issued a definitive statement.

Naturally the more tests there were the better the Bombs got to be.

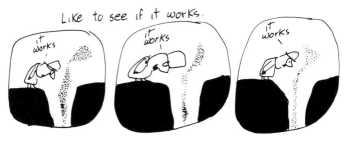

"THIS TEST HAS ADDED NO APPRECIABLE AMOUNT OF RADIO ACTIVE FALLOUT TO THE ATMOSPHERE"

"THIS IS LAST YEAR'S BOMB. WE THOUGHT IT WAS PRETTY ULTIMATE. REMEMBER?"

"BOY, WERE WE NAIVE!"

But the skies began to grow darker

and people noticed it and said:

"I GUESS THE GOVERNMENT MUST HAVE ITS SOUND REASONS."

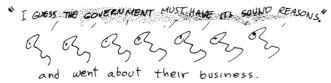

and went about their business.

Of course there was more going on than just Bomb tests. For instance, as soon as one country discovered a bigger Bomb than its neighbor

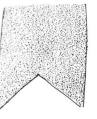

HA!

sigh

the first thing it did was call a disarmament conference—

and make a proposal-

"LETS ALL STOP WHERE WE ARE RIGHT NOW. ALL THOSE IN FAVOR OF PEACE SAY 'AYE!'"

and all the other countries replied: "WE AGREE. JUST AS SOON AS WE CATCH UP."

So there was a deadlock

and people heard the news and said:

"THATS THE WAY THE BALL BOUNCES"   or   "THATS THE WAY THE COOKIE CRUMBLES."

and went about their business.

But the conferences continued.

While more and more countries developed their own Bomb. And naturally all of them had to be invited.

and even some towns..

and even:

until every country had its own Bomb.

and people heard the news and said:

"THATS THE WAY THE ONION PEELS."

and went about their business.

Each test no matter how small, was carefully checked for after effects. "THIS TEST HAS ADDED NO APPRECIABLE AMOUNT OF RADIO ACTIVE FALLOUT TO THE ATMOSPHERE."

But now the skies began to look like this

and people noticed it and said:

"OF COURSE I'M CONCERNED BUT WHAT CAN ONE PERSON DO?"

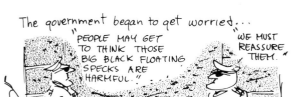

and went about their business.

The government began to get worried...

"PEOPLE MAY GET TO THINK THOSE BIG BLACK FLOATING SPECKS ARE HARMFUL."

"WE MUST REASSURE THEM."

So they hired a public relations outfit...

BIG BLACK FLOATING SPECKS ARE VERY PRETTY!

BIG BLACK FLOATING SPECKS ARE GOOD FOR YOU!

which put on a big campaign.

But the campaign had no effect. People got more and more concerned.

"ALL I DREAM ABOUT IS BIG BLACK FLOATING SPECKS."

"ADJUST TO IT."

Then the public relations outfit changed its tactics.

WHAT'S COMING?

IT'S COMING!

WHEN IS IT COMING?

SOON!

YEAH— BUT WHEN?

IT'S HERE!

WHAT?

SPECK PROOF FILTERS! Get Yours Today!

The public responded sympathetically. "WE'RE ON THE RIGHT TRACK AT LAST" said the public relations outfit.

BIG BLACK FLOATING SPECK PROOF TRANQUILIZERS

BIG BLACK FLOATING SPECK FILTERS

BIG BLACK FLOATING SPECK PROOF EYE GLASSES

Industry thrived.

World economy boomed.

The problem of over-population seemed somehow to diminish.

BASH

With the thickening of the specks, new businesses were born. The world grew rich. Education prospered. Art flourished.

It was a new renaissance

the other half worked on salves, medication, and storm windows.

Then one day...

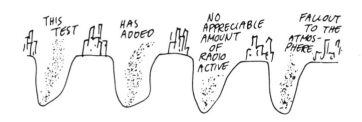

"GENTLEMEN, I MAY BE TALKING OFF THE TOP OF MY HEAD - BUT I THINK I'VE DREAMED UP A BOMB THAT WILL BLOW UP THE WHOLE WORKS!"

So the men on the inside got together—

"THIS DETERRENT WILL NEVER BE EFFECTIVE UNTIL WE TEST IT!"

But nobody wanted to take the blame. "HEY!" said somebody, "WHY DON'T WE TAKE THE QUESTION TO THE PEOPLE!"

Men on the inside campaigned vigorously.

THIS TEST WILL ADD NO APPRECIABLE AMOUNT OF RADIOACTIVE FALLOUT TO THE ATMOSPHERE.

But soon countries grew fat and complacent. Bomb production dropped off. And then - one day - the black specks began to disappear.

ITS HIGH TIME WE HAD NEW TESTS!

So while half the people in the world worked on new improved Bombs—

And people saw the situation and said:

"THATS THE WAY THE SPEARMINT CHEWS."—

and went about their business.

"WHAT A DETERRENT FOR PEACE" said men on the inside.

But propagandists in other countries planted seeds of doubt.

So it was decided. A referendum was announced.

STAND BEHIND YOUR GOVERNMENT. IT KNOWS WHATS BEST!

The test was given an overwhelming mandate. the people said:

"NOW IS NO TIME TO SHOW LACK OF UNITY."

and they went about their business.

So they had the test.

BOOM

and it worked.

A DANCE TO THE LOSS OF INNOCENCE.

IN THIS DANCE I HAVE SYMBOLIZED YOUTH, ITS HOPES, ITS WISHES, ITS DREAMS, ITS CHOICE OF FRIENDS, OF LOVERS, OF GODS.

YOUTH - BRIGHT AND EAGER TO SEARCH LIFE FOR ITS MEANING - CERTAIN IN THE KNOWLEDGE THAT IT WILL FIND THAT MEANING.

AND THEN COMES DISILLUSION.

THE DISAPPOINTMENT OF FRIENDS - THE INADEQUACY OF LOVERS - THE FAILURE OF GODS.

THE GAINING OF BITTER INSIGHTS - THERE IS NO ONE WHO DOESN'T LIE - THERE IS NOTHING INCORRUPTIBLE.

THEY'RE ALL CHEATS AND OUT TO GET YOU! DON'T BELIEVE A SINGLE ONE OF THE NO GOOD DIRTY —

FORGET IT —

I DON'T **FEEL** LIKE DANCING.

ALL MY DAYS ARE SPENT REWRITING HISTORY.

WHEN I WAS AN ADOLESCENT I WASN'T HAPPY WITH MY CHILDHOOD SO I REWROTE IT. AND IT SEEMED A LOT HAPPIER. WHEN I WAS A YOUNG MAN I REWROTE MY ADOLESCENCE.

I HAD MY FIRST ROMANCE AT SIXTEEN. IT TURNED OUT BADLY. I REWROTE IT. I'VE REWRITTEN EVERY ROMANCE SINCE - SOME AFTER FAVORITE NOVELS, SOME AFTER SOGGY MOVIES.

I REWRITE MY MARRIAGE CONSTANTLY. EACH TIME IT COMES OUT A LITTLE BETTER. SOME DAY I MAY HAVE IT DOWN PERFECT.

MY EXPERIENCES IN THE MORNING ARE REWRITTEN TO LOOK BETTER IN THE AFTERNOON. AT NIGHT I GO HOME, HAVE A DRINK, AND REWRITE THE WHOLE DAY.

ANYTHING NEW THAT HAPPENS TO ME IS ANALYZED BY THE KNOWLEDGE I'VE GAINED FROM THE PAST - REMEMBERED AS I REWROTE IT YEARS AGO.

AT FORTY I AM HAPPILY MARRIED - HAVE THREE LOVELY CHILDREN - A HOME IN THE SUBURBS - AND EXCELLENT PROSPECTS FOR JOB ADVANCEMENT.

NOBODY KNOWS IT BUT I'M A COMPLETE WORK OF FICTION.

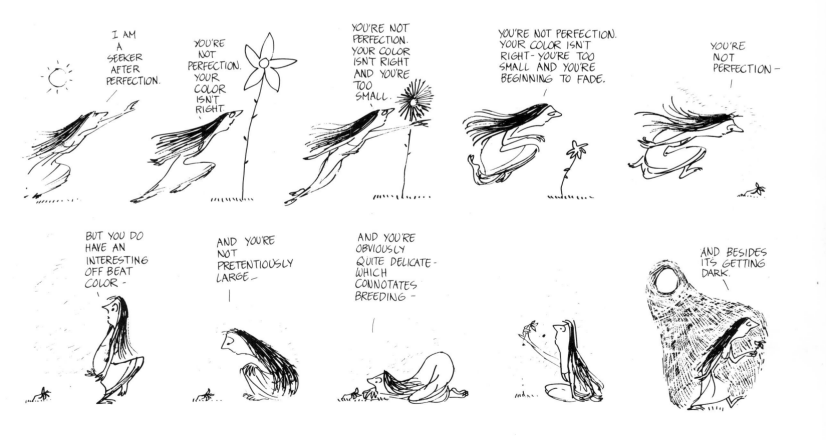

TODAY'S BOOK IS A RATHER BULKY BUT PROMISING FIRST ATTEMPT BY AUTHOR OR AUTHORS UNKNOWN.

IT'S CALLED THE BIBLE.

IT IS WRITTEN IN A NARRATIVE RATHER THAN INTROSPECTIVE STYLE WHICH MAY PERHAPS MAKE FOR QUICKER READING BUT LEAVES SOMETHING TO BE DESIRED ON THE LEVEL OF CHARACTER MOTIVATION.

IT PURPORTS TO BE A THEOLOGICAL AND HISTORICAL DOCUMENT, AND WHILE THIS REVIEWER DOES NOT QUESTION ITS SINCERITY, HE CAN ONLY REGRET THE PUBLISHER'S FAILURE TO INCLUDE A BIBLIOGRAPHY.

BUT THESE ARE MINOR CRITICISMS. ONE CAN NOT DENY THE POWER AND SWEEPING RANGE OF THE SUBJECT MATTER - (ONE MIGHT EVEN CALL IT EPIC) —

- THE SUBTLE ALLEGORICAL NUANCES TOUCHED, AT TIMES, WITH WHAT SEEMS TO BE AN ALMOST METAPHYSICAL INSIGHT! IT WILL UNDOUBTEDLY CAUSE CONTROVERSY IN THE LITERARY FIELD.

BUT THE AUTHORS, WHILE WRITING IN A QUASI-JOURNALISTIC FORM SHOW OCCASIONAL FLOURISHES OF STYLISTIC DARING WHICH MAKES ONE IMPATIENT TO VIEW THEIR LATER EFFORTS.

I SHALL AWAIT THEIR SECOND BOOK WITH GREAT INTEREST.

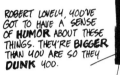

NOW LISTEN TO ME. **ALWAYS** LOOK OUT FOR YOURSELF. YOU LOOK OUT TOO MUCH FOR THE **OTHER** FELLOW AND WHEN **HE** GETS TO THE TOP HE'LL ONLY KICK YOU IN THE TEETH FOR THANKS.

O.K., DAD.

NOW **LISTEN** TO ME. LEARN TO BE WATCHFUL. NEVER TRUST ANYBODY—NOT EVEN ME! THE WORLD'S OUT TO **GET YOU**.

O.K., DAD.

NOW LISTEN TO ME. DEVELOP SINCERITY. LEARN A STRONG HANDSHAKE AND A GOOD EYE STARE. ALWAYS BE ATTENTIVE TO STRANGERS. THEY MIGHT DO YOU SOME GOOD.

O.K., DAD.

NOW LISTEN TO ME. DON'T **EVER** FEEL SORRY FOR YOURSELF. YOU'RE EATING GOOD AND YOU'VE ALWAYS GOT A CHANCE. WITH THE RIGHT MENTAL ATTITUDE YOU CAN TAKE **ANYBODY**.

O.K., DAD.

NOW FOR CRYING OUT LOUD, **LISTEN** TO ME. DON'T DO FAVORS! DON'T BE A PATSY! THE **SMART** GUYS **LAUGH** AT THE NICE GUYS. NEVER EXPECT TOO MUCH AND YOU WON'T BE DISAPPOINTED.

O.K., DAD.

WILL YOU **PLEASE** LISTEN TO ME. **NEVER** TALK POLITICS. YOU ONLY MAKE ENEMIES AND NOTHING **YOU'RE** GONNA SAY WILL EVER CHANGE THE WORLD.

O.K., DAD.

C'MON NOW YOU'RE NOT **LISTENING** TO ME. RESPECT **EVERY** GIRL LIKE SHE WAS YOUR MOTHER. BUT WHEN YOU **GOT** TO FOOL AROUND DO IT OUT OF THE NEIGHBORHOOD. NEVER PLAY IN YOUR OWN BACKYARD.

O.K., DAD.

YESSIR, WE'LL PUT OUR HEADS TOGETHER AND MAKE A MAN OUT OF YOU. YOU LISTENING, BOY?

O.K., DAD.

GOD— DON'T YOU JUST **HATE** THIS **RAT RACE**?

GOD YES.

HI JEANNIE! HI FAY!

HI RICK! HI CHUCK!

GOD— ALL THIS BLANKET HOPPING. ALL THIS PARTYING —

GOD— ISN'T IT A **DRAG**?

HI BETSY! HI BOBBY! HI FRAN!

HI PETE! HI FRED! HI STAN!

DON'T THEY EVER **LET UP**? WHAT ARE THEY **OVER** COMPENSATING FOR?

GOD ISN'T IT TOO **ADLERIAN**?

HI FRITZI! HI ROZ! HI CANDY! HI BEV! HI GIGI! HI DOT!

HI ROCK! HI DEAN! HI BUZZ! HI LEE! HI RED! HI BILLIE!

HOW I'LL **EVER** GET THROUGH LABOR DAY IS BEYOND ME. HOW OFTEN DO YOU COME OUT?

EVERY WEEKEND

HI FLO! HI GAIL! HI LILA! HI JANE! HI DORIS! HI SUE! HI MAY! HI PEG! HI EVE!

HI GRANT! HI JER! HI BUDDY! HI PHIL! HI NEIL! HI LOU! HI SPENCE! HI TIGE! HI RON!

THEY LEAD SUCH **EMPTY** LIVES.

HI CASEY! HI MARK! HI TOBY! HI FRANZ! HI SAL! HI KENT! HI ANDRE'! HI NAT····

 I MEET A GIRL AND I BUY HER THINGS AND SHE REJECTS ME AND **WHAT** DO I SAY?

 I SAY— "THIS WAS AN UNHEALTHY RELATIONSHIP BUT I HAVE LEARNED FROM IT."

SO I MEET **ANOTHER** GIRL AND SHE'S DIFFERENT AND I BUY HER THINGS AND SHE REJECTS ME AND **WHAT** DO I SAY?

 I SAY— "THIS WAS AN UNHEALTHY RELATIONSHIP BUT IT HAS **MATURED** ME."

 THEN I MEET A NEW GIRL WHO'S THE BEST YET AND I BUY HER THINGS AND SHE REJECTS ME AND WHAT, OH WHAT DO I SAY?

 I SAY— "THIS WAS AN UNHEALTHY RELATIONSHIP BUT IT HAS GIVEN ME INSIGHT."

 TIME AFTER TIME FOLLOWING EACH REJECTION I TELL MYSELF I'M **WISER** IN KNOWLEGE I'M **WISER** IN EXPERIENCE, I'M **WISER** IN DEPTH.

 I'VE COME TO LOOK ON MYSELF AS THE RENAISSANCE MAN OF THE REJECTEES.

SOMETIMES I WISH I WERE A **DICTATOR!**

A RULER.... A STRONG MAN... A **TITAN**...

WITH A RUTHLESS GRASP ON POWER AND AN IRON GRIP ON THE HELM OF GOVERNMENT!

—BUT LOVED.

THE LAW IS **MY** LAW. THE PEOPLE ARE **MY** PEOPLE. WHOMEVER I CONQUER **REMAINS** CONQUERED!

PREMIER BERNARD. **KING** BERNARD. **EMPEROR** BERNARD. **CZAR** BERNARD.

BOY.

THEN COULD I MEET GIRLS!

A
DANCE
TO
THE
END
OF
SUMMER.

IN THIS
DANCE
I HAVE
SYMBOLIZED
THE
SUMMER
SOLSTICE
IN ITS
DECLENSION.

THE
TIDES-
THE
SAND-
THE
SEA-

THE SUMMER
FLOWERS -
THE SAND
PIPERS -
THE GOOD
FISHERFOLK.

INSECT
REPELLENT,
THE MAIN
BOARDWALK,
BABY OIL.

ALL ARE GATHERED
IN AN ORGANIC
UNITY. ALL
TESTIFY TO
MAN AND
NATURE
BEING
AS ONE.

WHAT'S
SHE
DOING
THAT
FOR?

TO
LOSE
WEIGHT.

SOMETIMES
I FEEL
SMALL.

AND
SOMETIMES
I FEEL
LARGER -
THAN
LIFE.

SOMETIMES
I FEEL
CRUSHED.

AND SOMETIMES
I FEEL LIKE
A KING.

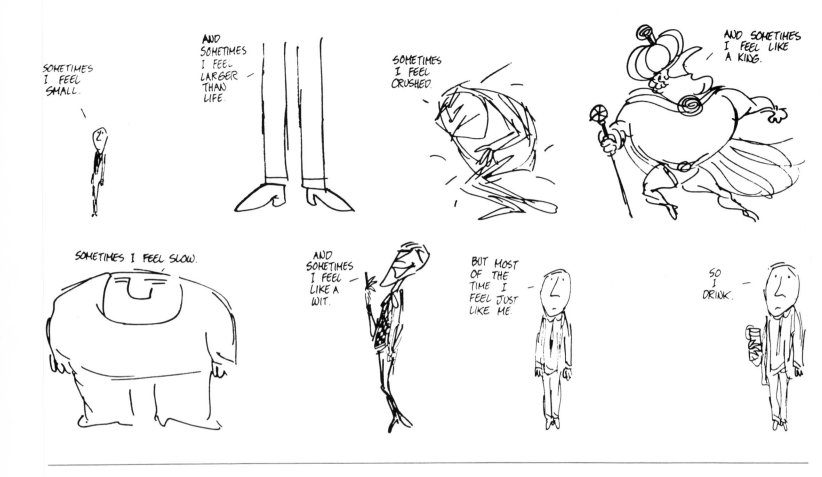

SOMETIMES I FEEL SLOW.

AND
SOMETIMES
I FEEL
LIKE A
WIT.

BUT MOST
OF THE
TIME I
FEEL JUST
LIKE ME.

SO
I
DRINK.

THE COMPANY'S
BEEN VERY
GOOD TO ME
SINCE I
GOT OUT OF
SCHOOL.

FIRST THEY ENROLLED
ME IN THEIR EXECUTIVE
TRAINING SQUAD—
LEARNING ALL PARTS
OF THE FIELD AND
GETTING PAID FOR
IT AS WELL.

THEN THEY HELPED
EVELYN AND ME
FIND A HOUSE
CONVENIENTLY
LOCATED IN A
SECTION WHERE
OTHER YOUNG
EXECUTIVES
LIVE—

AND WHEN EVELYN
BECAME ILL SMACK
DAB IN THE MIDDLE
OF HER TWENTY FIRST
BIRTHDAY PARTY THEY
ALLOWED US FULL
BENEFIT OF THE
COMPANY'S HOSP-
ITALIZATION PLAN
EVEN **THOUGH** I
WAS A MONTH
SHORT ON
ELIGIBILITY—

—AND IN SPITE
OF MY LOW SCORE
ON THE MONTHLY
PROMOTIONAL
EMOTIONAL QUIZ
AND SUBSEQUENT
DAILY MAKE UP
SESSIONS WITH
THE MORALE
DEPARTMENT'S
PSYCHOANALYST.

THEN WHEN, BECAUSE OF
EVELYN'S DRINKING
PROBLEM, IT LOOKED
LIKE I MIGHT BE
CASHIERED, THE EMER-
GENCY AID COMMITTEE
OF THE COMPANY'S
FAMILY COUNSELING
PLAN PLUS THE WIVE'S
AUXILIARY'S "BE A
PAL" SERVICE HELPED
PULL US THROUGH.

NOW THE LITTLE
WOMAN AND I ARE
BACK IN STEP. HERE
I AM ONLY TWENTY-
FOUR AND ALREADY
A SECOND CONSULT-
ATION ASSISTANT.
AND JUST YESTER-
DAY EVELYN
ENROLLED OUR THREE
YEAR OLD IN THE
EXECUTIVE JUNIORS
TRAINING SQUAD.

I COULD
DIE FOR
THE
COMPANY.

GO AHEAD! **EAT** ME! PLAY INTO **THEIR** HANDS.

PLEASE. MUST WE CONTINUALLY BICKER? CAN'T WE JUST ACCEPT OUR GIVEN ROLES?

OF COURSE, **YOU'D** SAY THAT. REFUSAL TO CHANGE IS A CHARACTERISTIC OF YOUR CLASS.

LOOK. I'M NOT AGAINST INTELLIGENT CHANGE. BUT THIS QUESTION HAS BEEN LOOKED INTO BEFORE. CATS HAVE **ALWAYS** KILLED MICE. IT'S A TRADITION.

AN OUTMODED RITUAL UNFIT FOR TODAY'S HUMANISTIC VALUES. DON'T YOU SEE WHO PROFITS MOST FROM THE UNNATURAL ENMITY BETWEEN OUR PEOPLES?

YOUR KIND ALWAYS HAS TO LOOK FOR VILLAINS. IT BORES ME.

HOW INCREDIBLY NAIVE! WHOSE ENDS DO YOU **REALLY** SERVE? WHO GAINS BY DIVERTING BOTH OF US INTO A **USELESS** STRUGGLE THAT CAN'T **EVER** END?

:SIGH: I SUPPOSE YOU'LL TELL ME WHETHER I WANT TO HEAR OR NOT.

IT'S **MAN**! YOU SILLY INNOCENT! **MAN**!

OH, COME NOW. MAN PETS ME. MAN GIVES ME FOOD.

SHEER PATERNALISM YOU BOOBY! HOW ELSE CAN HE KEEP HIS WANING POWER?

YOU ALWAYS MAKE ME UNCOMFORTABLE WITH THAT KIND OF TALK.

WE MICE HAVE BEEN PLAYING A WAITING GAME! MAN IS TORN BY INNER DISSENSION. LET MOUSE AND CAT JOIN HANDS AGAINST THE COMMON ENEMY! **UNITE! UNITE!**

QUIET— SOMEBODY MIGHT HEAR—

I SEE MY WORDS ARE WASTED. ALL RIGHT THEN— **EAT** ME. GO AHEAD.

I CAN'T. YOU'VE MADE ME ALL UPSET. I'VE GOT A STOMACH ACHE.

I'LL BE BACK LATER. MAYBE I'LL EAT YOU THEN.

WEAKLING— WISHYWASHY— I WOULD HAVE EATEN **HIM**

WHAT CAN YOU EXPECT FROM LIBERALS.

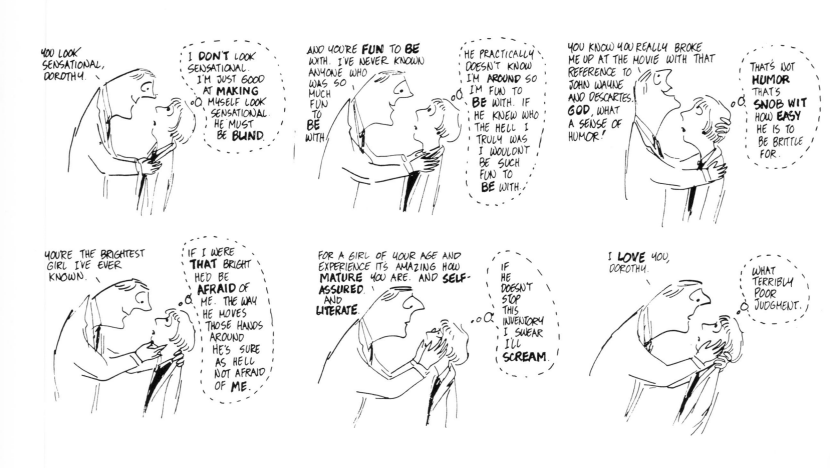

I'VE QUIT GOING OUT.

WHAT IS THIS YOU'VE QUIT GOING OUT BIT? HOW CAN YOU QUIT GOING OUT?

I'VE JUST **QUIT**, THAT'S ALL. IT'S DISHONEST AND I'M THROUGH. THE **HELL** WITH IT!

DIS**HONEST**? WHAT DO YOU MEAN DIS**HONEST**?

ALRIGHT. A WEEK AGO I'M ASLEEP IN BED- TWO IN THE MORNING- AND THE **PHONE** RINGS- THE **SEXIEST** VOICE I'VE EVER HEARD!

SHE SAYS HER NAME IS **DARLENE** AND SHE JUST FLEW IN FROM THE COAST AND SHE'S A FRIEND OF A FRIEND AND SHE HAS NO PLACE TO STAY AND CAN I PUT HER UP FOR THE NIGHT.

ALRIGHT. I KNOW **SOMETHING** MUST BE WRONG - BUT I TELL HER TO COME OVER. AN HOUR LATER SHE ARRIVES. **THE MOST BEAUTIFUL GIRL I HAVE EVER SEEN!** AND IN SHE COMES WITH TWO BOTTLES OF BRANDY AND A DOZEN EGGS.

SHE WHIPS UP THE MOST **FABULOUS** BREAKFAST I'VE EVER TASTED. WE SIT AND TALK FOR **HOURS**. SHE'S READ **ALL** THE BOOKS I'VE READ- LOVES **ALL** THE MUSIC I LOVE - THE **BRIGHT- EST**, MOST **SEN- SITIVE** GIRL I'VE EVER KNOWN!

ALONG TOWARD DAWN WE BEGIN TO NUZZLE A LITTLE. I BUILD A FIRE. SUDDENLY WE'RE **GRABBING** EACH OTHER! WARM? YOU WOULDN'T BELIEVE IT! AFFECTIONATE? YOU HAVE **NO** CONCEPTION!

IT WAS THE LOVELIEST, PUREST EXPERIENCE I EVER HOPE TO HAVE - A FANTASY COME **TRUE** - ME WITH THE MOST BEAUTIFUL, DELIGHTFUL GIRL IN THE WORLD - AND SHE **LOVES** ME! SHE LOVES ME!

AND ALL THAT TIME DO YOU KNOW WHAT I WAS THINKING?

WHAT?

"WAIT TILL I TELL THE FELLAS."

I BELIEVE SENATOR KENNEDY BELIEVES WHAT HE BELIEVES SINCERELY AS I BELIEVE THAT I BELIEVE WHAT I BELIEVE SINCERELY.

WHAT DO I MEAN BY "SINCERELY"? **THIS** IS WHAT I MEAN BY "SINCERELY." I MEAN THAT BOTH OF US ARE HONEST IN OUR FEELINGS ABOUT OUR DIFFERENCES IN APPROACH TO WHAT IS BEST FOR OUR NATION'S FUTURE.

WHAT DO I MEAN BY "APPROACH TO"? **THIS** IS WHAT I MEAN BY "APPROACH TO." I MEAN THAT IN THE WORDS OF JEFFERSON - "THAT GOVERNMENT IS BEST WHICH GOVERNS LEAST." NOW WHAT DID JEFFERSON MEAN BY "LEAST"? **THIS** IS WHAT I BELIEVE JEFFERSON MEANT BY "LEAST."

SENATOR KENNEDY MAY DISAGREE WITH ME IN MY INTERPRETATION. I HAVE NO DOUBT HE WILL BE SINCERE IN HIS DISAGREEMENT WITH MY INTERPRETATION AS I AM SINCERE IN MY AGREEMENT WITH MY INTERPRETATION. MORE ABOUT THAT LATER! WHAT DO I MEAN BY "LATER?"

I MEAN THAT WHILE MR. KHRUSHCHEV IS IN THIS COUNTRY IT IS NOT IN THE BEST INTERESTS OF THE AMERICAN PEOPLE TO SHOW OUR DISSENSION OR LACK OF FAITH IN OUR SYSTEM, ALTHOUGH I FEEL THAT MR. KHRUSHCHEV (AND I HAVE TOLD HIM THIS POINT BLANK) IS SINCERE IN HIS LACK OF FAITH IN OUR SYSTEM.

WHAT DO I MEAN BY "SINCERE," "FAITH," "OUR" AND "SYSTEM"? **THIS** IS WHAT I MEAN BY—

NOW THE QUESTION IS **THIS:** NUMBER ONE - ARE WE DOING ALL WE CAN ABOUT CUBA? NUMBER ONE-a - I DON'T BELIEVE WE **ARE!** NUMBER TWO- IN A WHITE PAPER LARST WEEK I SUGGESTED THAT WE SHOULD DO **ALL** IN OUR POWER TO OVERTHROW THE CUBAN GOVERNMENT BE- CAUSE ITS AN UNFRIENDLY DAGGER JUST OFF OUR COAST.

NUMBER TWO-a - MR. NIXON DIS- AGREES. NUMBER TWO-a, ROMAN NUMERAL I - HE VIEWS THIS AS A VERY DANGEROUS POLICY. NUMBER TWO-a, ROMAN NUMERAL II - HE WANTS US, INSTEAD, TO TAKE THE **SAME** STAND ON CUBA AS WE DID ON GUATEMALA.

i.e. - DO **ALL** IN OUR POWER TO OVERTHROW THE GUATEMALAN GOVERNMENT BECAUSE IT WAS AN UNFRIENDLY DAGGER JUST OFF OUR COAST. NUMBER THREE, ROMAN NUMERAL IV, V, AND VI - I BELIEVE THIS TO BE AN **EVASIVE** POLICY.

BUT- NEW PARAGRAPH, NUMBER ONE-a - MR. NIXON **DOES** AGREE THAT WE **SHOULD** DEFEND FORMOSA - WHICH IS OUR **FRIENDLY** DAGGER JUST OFF THE CHINA COAST. NUMBER ONE-b - I DON'T BELIEVE THAT'S **ENOUGH.**

NUMBER TWO STROKE THREE, PART ONE - I BELIEVE WE MUST DO FAR **MORE.** WE MUST GAIN FOR OURSELVES THE FRIENDSHIP OF ALL THE **EMERGING, UN- COMMITTED** DAGGERS IN ASIA AND AFRICA. HERE, ROMAN NUMERALS M THROUGH MCV, IS OUR AREA OF DISAGREEMENT.

IN MY NEXT REBUTTAL, FOLLOWING THE COUNT DOWN, I'D LIKE TO DISCUSS MY PROGRAM FOR THE AGED.

NOW YOU TAKE REBELLION. WHEN I WAS A KID WE USED TO HAVE **REBELLION!**

DARN RIGHT! WE'VE SOLD OUT OUR IN- TEGRITY FOR A MESS OF STATUS. THAT'S OUR TROUBLE.

WHEN WAS THE LAST TIME YOU SAW A COLLEGE KID WITH A PICKET SIGN? WE'VE LOST THE URGE TO **DEFY!**

IT'S A CON- FORMIST CULTURE. THAT'S **OUR** TROUBLE.

SMALL, FRIGHT- ENED PEOPLE, **THAT'S** WHAT WE ALL ARE!

TRAPPED BY KEROUAC ON THE LEFT AND "THE NEW YORKER" ON THE RIGHT. THAT'S OUR TROUBLE.

WHAT IF EVERY COPY WRITER IN THE CITY WOKE UP ONE MORN- ING AND **REFUSED** TO GO IN TO HIS AGENCY?

WHAT A **GREAT** CONCEPT!

FOR **WEEKS** NOT **ONE** SINGLE LINE OF COPY WOULD BE WRITTEN!

THE **ECONOMY** WOULD BREAK DOWN! THE GOVERNMENT WOULD HAVE TO **NATIONALIZE** THE ADVER- TISING FIELD!

A REBELLION OF THE **CONFORMISTS!**

THE LOWEST COMMON DENOMINATOR STRIKES BACK!

LET'S BEGIN ON A MANIFESTO IMMED- IATELY! I CAN PUT ASIDE MY NOVEL AND WORK NIGHTS!

"TRUTH TO THE PRINTED PAGE" SHALL BE OUR WATCHWORD!

WELL, LET'S NOT OVER **STIMULATE.** WE WOULDN'T WANT TO ALIENATE OUR MARKET.

HERE COMES THE COFFEE WAGON. LET'S TALK MORE TOMORROW.

THE SUNDANCE KID

Kennedy blew into our lives like a blast of cool air, bracing us where Ike had pacified us, replacing age with youth, ending our apathy with a rhetoric that mixed pugnaciousness with hope. He acted out a style of charged glamor, Cary Grant in the White House, our first movie star president. It pleased us to see a president give a performance for the press, to beat them, not by lulling reporters to sleep but by making them chuckle and genuflect. He was nothing but charm. Style engulfed substance. Not that he didn't have beliefs; they started with self and flared outward. His style was Teddy Roosevelt macho; the concept of limited conventional warfare replaced the scarier scheme of massive retaliation: small-scale non-nuclear wars against manageable non-white countries. Our fear of the ultimate weapon put aside, the country got moving again.

His views on foreign affairs were shaped by James Bond: He adored code, covert operations, counterinsurgency, Green Berets. He charged into Cuba, was beaten off, charged back again, this time behind the scenes, held the world hostage in a missile crisis, sent the first combat troops into Vietnam. At home, he was ineffectual with Congress, uncaring on civil liberties, duplicitous on civil rights—but he was gorgeous and he had class. My friends loved the rumors that he slept around, screwed movie stars, kept an ambassador's wife in the Carlyle Hotel. The cocksman president. What a fantasy for Bernard Mergendeiler! Dissent was welcomed back to the body politic. Kennedy didn't mind it as Eisenhower and his minions had. Kennedy patronized dissent. He was rich and Harvard educated, he understood about most liberals: Invite them to dinner at the White House; dazzled by the attention they will behave.

The Kennedy liberals called themselves pragmatic, tough-minded decision makers. They had taken over from the Stevenson liberals whom they described as weak-kneed and wooly-minded. Stevenson liberals, they said, couldn't get it up. If they could get it up, it certainly wouldn't stay up long enough to stick it to the enemy. The New Frontiersmen not only got it up, they talked about how up it was. They compared their degree of up to the upness of the other side. No accident that sexual liberation and Lenny Bruce's comedy came into fashion at this time. It began as political metaphor.

Sex was good. The Pill was good. A meaningful relationship, that '50s hangover, was still good. Communication was good. A breakdown in communication was bad, as were alienation, behavior modification, motivational research, popular culture, and ad men. French movies and Italian movies were better than American movies, but English movies, which used to be good, were not that good anymore. Leisure was not as worrisome a problem as it had been. Educating the gifted child was a problem. The pursuit of excellence was a goal.

Art and culture made it to the White House, first time in years. Andy Warhol was invented; who would have known of him had Nixon been elected? The Beautiful People emerged. Intellectuals were in fashion. Book reviewers visited the White House, talked literary criticism and politics with the president; keep in touch, he said. Secret CIA endowments continued to fund academic journals and scholars. Poets and critics blossomed into media figures. Several got tenure at Camelot.

Non-violent demonstrations in the South introduced a style of protest that spread north, from civil rights to peace marches. Poverty turned up, discovered by Michael Harrington in his book, *The Other America*, reviewed in a long essay in *The New Yorker*. The president was in awe of *The New Yorker*. Once the magazine recognized poverty, it behooved him to invite it to dinner. Headstart and other programs followed. If *The New Yorker* had come out early enough against Vietnam, Kennedy might have saved us a war.

In drawing him, his good looks plagued me. I studied photographs and the television screen, concluding always after my unsatisfactory caricatures, "I can do bett*ah.*" But he aged fast in office. His features thickened, his jaw heavied, he developed jowls. By the time he died, I was onto him.

A DANCE TO THE NEW YEAR.

IN THIS DANCE I HAVE SYMBOLIZED PEACE ON EARTH AND GOOD WILL TO ALL MEN.

UM- I DON'T WANT YOU TO THINK I MEAN ANYTHING **FUNNY** BY THAT STATEMENT- I MEAN PEACE, YES- BUT WITHOUT APPEASE- MENT ON THE AFOREMENTIONED EARTH AND, NATURALLY, GOOD WILL TO ALL MEN.

UH-WAIT A MINUTE- BY GOOD WILL I MEAN THAT WE SHOULD HAVE GOOD WILL TO THOSE WHO ARE- YOU KNOW- ALL MEN OF GOOD WILL -

WAIT A MINUTE- BY **ALL** MEN I MEAN ONLY **THOSE** MEN WHOM WE RECOGNIZE AS WILLING TO BE **REASONABLE** AND SEE OUR SIDE AS WELL AS THEIR OWN-AS LONG AS THEY DON'T HAVE A DOUBLE STANDARD AND PRETEND TO BE NEUTRALISTS.

SO REALLY WHAT THIS DANCE SYMBOLIZES IS A **RESPONSIBLE, CAUTIOUS** APPROACH-

TO ARMS CONTROL ON EARTH AND FRUITFUL NEGOTIATION TO SOME MEN.

I CALL IT "THE BENDS."

GENTLEMEN, IF YOU WILL, PLEASE TURN TO PP. 42 OF THE APPENDIX: WHITE PAPER NUMBER 6521, PAR. 14. DO YOU ALL HAVE IT?

RE: RIVALRY— **CIA** VS. **STATE**? IS THAT IT, CHIEF?

YES, NOW, PIERRE, IF YOU WILL SUMMAR- IZE—

EXCUSE IT, CHIEF. HERE'S CHESTER.

SORRY I'M LATE, CHIEF. I WAS FINISHING UP A BOOK REVIEW.

TRY TO BE PROMPT, CHESTER. THE REST OF US MANAGE TO GET OUR BOOK REVIEWS DONE ON OUR **OWN** TIME.

PSST, ARTHUR! WHAT'S THE PAGE?

PP. 42, PAR. 14

NOW THEN, THE PROBLEM IS THE IMPROVEMENT OF INTELLIGENCE OPERATIONS BETWEEN OURSELVES AND **RUSSIER**, OUR-SELVES AND **ASIER**, AND (MORE DIFFICULT BECAUSE IT'S A CLOSED SOCIETY) OURSELVES AND **CIA**. YES, ED—

WELL, WE'VE HAD SOME SUCCESS IN TRACKING CIA'S AC-TIVITIES BY MONITORING THE ENEMY'S RADIO ACCUSATIONS, CHIEF.

TRUE. HOWEVER **STATE** TELLS ME IT FINDS IT INCREASINGLY FRUSTRATING TO RECOGNIZE A **NEW** GOVERNMENT IN THE **MORNING** ONLY TO HAVE **CIA** TRY TO OVERTHROW IT IN THE **AFTERNOON**. NOW, THAT'S **SLOPPY**.

IN TERMS OF LONG RANGE PLANNING **CIA** SHOULD, ON OCCASION, HAVE THE SAME FOREIGN POLICY AS **STATE**, WOULDN'T YOU SAY, CHIEF?

I'LL BUY THAT, WALT. TYPE UP A CLASSIFIED MEMO AND LEAK IT TO THE PRESS. NOW AFTER LUNCH I WANT TO DISCUSS POSSIBLE SITES FOR A FUTURE SERIES OF ATMOS-PHERIC TESTS. I UNDERSTAND THAT SOMEBODY SUGGESTED HAVANA.

BON APPETIT, CHIEF

LIKE EVERYBODY ELSE I WAS A SOCIALIST WHEN I WAS IN COLLEGE DURING THE TWENTIES— "SOLIDARITY FOREVER" "ORGANIZE THE WORKERS!" "OVERTHROW THE GOVERN-MENT!"

I WAS A LIBERAL WHEN I GOT OUT OF COLLEGE IN THE THIRTIES— "NEW DEAL RECOVERY" "DOWN WITH BOOM AND BUST" "UP THE C.I.O."

I WAS A COMMUNIST DURING THE FORTIES— "UNITED FRONT" "FREE EARL BROWDER" "JAIL THE TROTSKYITES."

I WAS A DUPE DURING THE FIFTIES— "BUT I DIDN'T REALIZE—" "THEY USED ME—" "I'LL NEVER SIGN ANYTHING AGAIN—"

AND NOW IN THE SIXTIES I'M A CONSERVATIVE— "KEEP RED CHINA OUT OF THE U.N." "OVERTHROW CUBA" "UP BARRY GOLDWATER."

IT'S GOOD TO SEE I'M STILL IN STEP WITH THE COLLEGE KIDS.

IN THE OLD DAYS I USED TO GET INVITED TO THESE PARTIES—YOU KNOW—WHERE THE HOSTESS INSISTED THEY **HAD** TO BE **INTEGRATED**—YOU KNOW? SO THEY'D INVITE **ME**.

AND I'D ALWAYS MEET A WHOLE BUNCH OF OFFICIAL-FRIENDLY PEOPLE—YOU KNOW—**GUYS** WITH **STRONG** HAND SHAKES, **CHICKS** WHO **HAD** TO DANCE WITH ME. IT'S NOT EASY BEING ROBBED OF A CHOICE WHEN THE GIRL IS UGLY.

AND SOONER OR LATER A COUPLE OF THESE CATS WOULD GET ME IN A CORNER AND—WE'D ALL BLOW SMOKE AT EACH OTHER AND BE **ENLIGHTENED**—AND THEY'D WANT TO TALK ABOUT CIVIL RIGHTS UNDER THE DEMOCRATS BECAUSE THERE'S NOTHING A LIBERAL LOVES BETTER THAN BEING MADE TO **FEEL GUILTY**—BUT I WOULDN'T **TOUCH** IT—I'D TALK ABOUT MY **CAR** AND **BASEBALL** AND HOW **DULL** FOREIGN MOVIES ARE.

UNTIL THEY GOT SO JUMPY THAT **ONE** OF THEM **HAD** TO BRING "IT" UP. AND I'D PRETEND TO BE **SURPRISED** THAT THEY'D BE INTERESTED IN **MY** PROBLEMS. BUT THEY INSISTED THAT BEING MEMBERS OF THE **A.D.A.** THEY CONSIDERED IT **EVERYBODY'S** PROBLEM.

SO I ONLY SAID I DIDN'T **LOOK ON** CIVIL RIGHTS AS A "**HUMANIST**" ISSUE. THE WAY **I** LOOKED AT IT—IT WAS STRICTLY **SELF-INTEREST**. YOU KNOW—LIKE IT'S BEEN A LONG WAIT AND **I** WANT **MINE**.

SO A COUPLE OF THEM, HERE AND THERE, GOT **RESTLESS** ABOUT WHAT THEY CALLED MY "EXTREMIST" ATTITUDE. BUT ALL THE WHILE THEY KEPT **SMILING**. AS A PEOPLE I FIND LIBERALS VERY **GOOD NATURED**.

BUT THE PARTY ALWAYS BROKE UP ABOUT AN HOUR EARLY AND I COULD SEE **NOBODY** REALLY GOT WHAT THEY **CAME** FOR—EXCEPT ME. I FELT I WAS SUBTLY PUSHING A FASTER RATE OF SOCIAL INTEGRATION. AND I WAS **RIGHT**.

AT THEIR NEXT PARTY THEY HAD **TWO** NEGROES—JUST IN CASE THE FIRST ONE DIDN'T WORK OUT.

PARDON ME, SIR. WHY ARE YOU FOLLOWING ME?

I'M YOUR SIT IN.

YOU MUST HAVE THE WRONG PARTY.—**I'M** NOT A LUNCH COUNTER.

I'M A **SOCIAL** SIT IN, NOT A PROPERTY SIT IN. WE INTEGRATE **PEOPLE**.

DON'T GET ME WRONG. I UNDERSTAND WHAT YOU'RE TRYING TO DO. BUT I **CAN'T** TAKE YOU TO WORK WITH ME.

HAVE YOU EVER TAKEN A COLORED PERSON TO WORK WITH YOU?

BELIEVE ME, I WOULD IF I FOUND ONE QUALIFIED.—I'M ON **YOUR** SIDE. **YOU** DON'T WANT **ME**!

WONDERFUL. WE CAN DISCUSS IT AT WORK.

LOOK, I **DO** MY BIT! EVERY DAY I **DELIBERATELY** SIT NEXT TO ONE OF YOU ON THE BUS! DON'T I GET **SOME** TIME OFF FOR LIBERALISM?

HAVE YOU EVER TAKEN A COLORED PERSON HOME WITH YOU?

HOLD ON! I NEVER MIX MY HOME LIFE WITH MY POLITICS! HOW LONG DO YOU EXPECT TO STAY WITH ME?

WHITHER YOU GOEST, BABY, I GOEST.

CIVIL RIGHTS USED TO BE SO MUCH MORE TOLERABLE BEFORE NEGROES GOT INTO IT.

SO MOMMA AND I GOT ON THIS BUS TO GO TO THE COUNTRY AND SUDDENLY A BUNCH OF COLORED PEOPLE GOT ON AND WE WERE SURROUNDED BY POLICEMEN AND WE ALL GOT ARRESTED.

MOMMA **TRIED** TO TELL THE POLICEMEN WE WERE ONLY GOING TO THE COUNTRY BUT ALL THE COLORED PEOPLE WERE SINGING "**WE SHALL OVERCOME**" SO THE POLICEMEN COULDN'T HEAR US.

SO AFTER DADDY GOT US OUT OF JAIL MOMMA AND I WENT TO GET A **SANDWICH** IN A **DRUG-STORE** BEFORE WE TRIED AGAIN TO GO TO THE COUNTRY—AND SUDDENLY A BUNCH OF COLORED PEOPLE WERE SITTING ON STOOLS ALL AROUND US AND WE WERE SURROUNDED BY POLICEMEN AND WE ALL GOT ARRESTED.

MOMMA **TRIED** TO TELL THE POLICE-MEN WE WERE ONLY TRYING TO **EAT** AND **GO TO THE COUNTRY** BUT ALL THE COLORED PEOPLE WERE SINGING "**WE SHALL OVERCOME**" SO THE POLICEMEN COULDN'T HEAR US.

SO AFTER DADDY GOT US OUT OF JAIL WE **RENTED** A CAR TO THE COUNTRY AND MOMMA WAS SO RELIEVED THAT BEFORE EVEN **UNPACKING** SHE TOOK ME DOWN TO THE BEACH TO RELAX AND SUN BATHE AND SUDDENLY A BUNCH OF COLORED PEOPLE WERE SUN BATHING ALL AROUND US AND THE POLICEMEN CAME AND WE ALL GOT ARRESTED.

MOMMA **TRIED** TO TELL THE POLICE-MEN WE WERE ONLY TRYING TO SUN BATHE BUT ALL THE COLORED PEOPLE AND ME WERE SINGING "**WE SHALL OVERCOME**" SO THEY TOOK US TO JAIL.

I DON'T MIND THE COLORED PEOPLE BUT I WISH THEY'D LEAVE THEIR POLICEMEN HOME.

DON'T GIVE ME THAT HANDKERCHIEF-HEAD PACIFISM! IT'S TIME FOR THE 'AFRO-AMERICAN' TO MEET VIOLENCE WITH VIOLENCE!

NONSENSE! NON-VIOLENT RESISTANCE IS THE MOST EFFECTIVE WEAPON THE NEGRO **HAS**. WHY SURRENDER IT?

IF MISTER BOSS BUMPS YOU, YOU BUMP MISTER BOSS. ANYTHING LESS IS A **SELL OUT**! AFRO-AMERICANS HAD BETTER **KNOW** IT!

THAT'S THE BLOODY ROAD TO INTEGRATION. THAT'S **JUST** WHAT THE BIGOTS HOPE FOR!

THE BIGOTS AREN'T OUR **ONLY** ENEMY, MAN! SO'S YOUR GO-SLOW BUDDY THE WHITE LIBERAL!

THE NEGRO WILL WIN HIS RIGHTS **PEACEFULLY** OR NOT AT ALL! WE CAN'T AFFORD TO LOSE THE FRIENDS WE'VE MADE!

PEACE MEANS **WHITE** MAN'S PEACE. YOUR NON-VIOLENCE BETTER WORK **PRETTY** SOON, MAN! A **LOT** OF US ARE GETTING **DAMN** TIRED!

DID **YOU** HEAR **THAT**?

SHHH

WE'D BETTER INTEGRATE **IMMEDIATLY**!

GOD, **YES**! BEFORE THOSE **EXTREMISTS** TAKE OVER!

NICE WORK, CHARLIE.

THERE'S **ANOTHER** WHITE BAR DOWN THE BLOCK. LETS GO DOWN **THERE** AND PANIC THEM.

SO I SAID TO HIM: "YOU'RE ON THE WRONG TRACK, — PHIL. MAN IS **NOT** BASICALLY EVIL. MAN IS NEITHER BASICALLY **GOOD** NOR **EVIL**."

PERFECTLY REASONABLE.

I SAID TO HIM "YOU'RE **OVER-SIMPLIFYING** PHIL. NO ONE DENIES — THAT MAN COMMITS GREAT SINS. BUT **DON'T** JUST LOOK ON THE **DARK** SIDE. LOOK AT THE FORCE FOR **GOOD** HE'S BEEN."

PERFECTLY REASONABLE.

I SAID TO HIM: "YOU'RE **OVERLY ANALYTICAL**, PHIL. MAN DOESN'T DO GOOD TO ALLEVIATE SOME FANCIED SENSE OF GUILT — AS **YOU** THINK. WHEN MAN DOES GOOD ITS BECAUSE HE **IS** GOOD. WHEN MAN DOES EVIL ITS BECAUSE **SOCIETY** HAS MADE HIM THAT WAY."

PERFECTLY REASONABLE.

I SAID TO HIM: "YOU'RE TOO MUCH THE PESSIMIST, PHIL. CERTAINLY, WE MOVE **SLOWLY**, BUT IF **ALL** OF US IN OUR **OWN** LIVES — MAKE AS GOOD A JOB OF IT AS WE CAN — AS PARENTS, AS TEACHERS, AS BUSINESS MEN, AS CITIZENS — THEN LITTLE BY LITTLE THE WORLD **HAS** TO BECOME A BETTER PLACE TO LIVE IN."

PERFECTLY REASONABLE.

NOT ACCORDING TO **PHIL**. HE LAUGHED IN MY FACE AND — CALLED ME AN IDIOT-LIBERAL!

HOW AWFUL! WHAT DID YOU DO?

WHAT **COULD** I DO? — I KILLED HIM.

PERFECTLY REASONABLE.

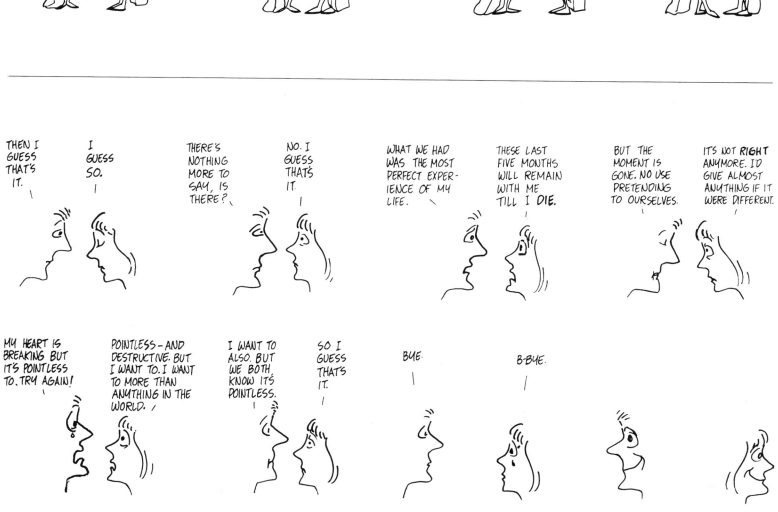

I USED TO WORK FOR THE F.B.I. - ASSIGNED TO THE PEACE MOVEMENT- UNDERGROUND AGENT TO CHECK OUT COMMUNIST INFILTRATION.

ALL PRETTY ROUTINE- MASS MEETINGS - PICKETING THE WHITE HOUSE- KENNEDY SERVING COFFEE - NO RESULTS WHATEVER -

THEN I MET EDNA- SOFT- COMPELLING- DOCTRINAIRE-. SHE FELL IN LOVE. I FELL IN LOVE. WE DECIDED ON MARRIAGE.

BUT MY SECRET SEPARATED US. I HAD TO TELL HER. I PROCEEDED TO DO SO. ON OUR WEDDING NIGHT I REPORTED "EDNA, I AM AN UNDERGROUND AGENT FOR YOUR F.B.I.

EDNA WEPT. THEN SHE TOLD ME **HER** SECRET. "SAM," SHE REPORTED, "I AM AN UNDERGROUND COMMUNIST ASSIGNED TO INFILTRATE THE PEACE MOVEMENT.

YOU CAN IMAGINE WHAT FOLLOWED. A LOVER'S QUARREL. I INSISTED EDNA GIVE UP **HER** WORK. SHE INSISTED I GIVE UP **MINE**.

WE CONSULTED A MARRIAGE COUNSELOR. HE ADVISED US TO COMPROMISE- "ALL FORMS OF EXTREMISM ARE MISGUIDED" HE REPORTED. "QUIT YOUR RESPECTIVE JOBS AND JOIN A COMMUNITY CENTER."

I COULDN'T. EDNA COULDN'T. WE SAID GOOD- BYE AND I TURNED HER IN.

I'LL ALWAYS WAIT FOR YOU EDNA

I ALWAYS USED TO NOTICE GIRLS ON THE BUS IF THEY WERE WRITING IN A NOTEBOOK.

I'D FIGURE THEY WERE **WRITERS** AND I'D WANT TO GO OVER AND START A CONVERSATION ABOUT HOW **I** USED TO WRITE A LOT IN SCHOOL—

AND I WAS GOING TO DO IT **AGAIN** SOMEDAY. AND THEY'D BE ABLE TO TELL FROM THE WAY I TALKED AND MY PERSONAL CHARM AND EVERYTHING THAT IF I EVER **WANTED** TO I **COULD** BE A VERY GOOD WRITER.

AND JUST TO SHOW THEM THAT I WASN'T A LOT OF HOT AIR I'D SAY **NAMES** TO THEM - LIKE "BELLOW" AND "MALAMUD" AND "ALBEE"- YOU KNOW, SO THEY'D BEGIN TO **TRUST** ME AND LET ME LOOK AT WHAT THEY HAD WRITTEN.

AND IT WOULD BE **GREAT!** REALLY **GREAT!** NOT QUITE AS GREAT AS WHAT **I** COULD WRITE IF I EVER GOT AROUND TO IT. LESS GREAT, BUT GREAT NEVERTHELESS.

AND I'D MAKE A FEW CRITICISMS- YOU KNOW, ABOUT **SENTENCE STRUC- TURE** - THINGS THAT WOULD SHOW I KNEW WHAT I WAS TALKING ABOUT.

AND WHEN THEY'D GET OFF THE BUS THEY'D BE **SURPRISED** BECAUSE INSTEAD OF GETTING OFF WITH THEM I'D SAY: "GOODBYE."

AND THEN THEY'D KNOW THAT I WASN'T JUST A **PHONEY** TRYING FOR A PICKUP AND THEY'D BE VERY IMPRESSED WITH ME.

AND **THAT'S** ALL I'D WANT.

I JUST WANT SOMEBODY TO BE IMPRESSED WITH ME.

BY THE TIME GEORGE TOLD ME HE WAS LEAVING ON A BUSINESS TRIP FOR A MONTH I HAD LOST ALL **FEELING** FOR HIM.

EACH DINNER WHEN HE'D COME HOME I'D TRY TO REKINDLE THE FLAME, BUT ALL I COULD THINK OF AS HE GOBBLED UP MY CHICKEN WAS: "ALL I AM IS A **SERVANT** TO YOU, GEORGE."

SO WHEN HE ANNOUNCED HE HAD TO GO AWAY I WAS **DELIGHTED.** WHILE GEORGE WAS AWAY I COULD **FIND** MY- SELF AGAIN! I COULD MAKE **PLANS!**

THE FIRST WEEK GEORGE WAS AWAY I WENT OUT SEVEN TIMES. THE TELEPHONE NEVER STOPPED RINGING. I HAD A **MARVELOUS** TIME!

THE SECOND WEEK GEORGE WAS AWAY I GOT **TIRED** OF THE SAME OLD FACES, SAME OLD LINES. I REMEMBERED WHAT DROVE ME TO MARRY GEORGE IN THE FIRST PLACE.

THE THIRD WEEK GEORGE WAS AWAY I FELT CLOSER TO HIM THAN I HAD IN **YEARS.** I STAYED HOME, READ JANE AUSTEN AND SLEPT ON GEORGE'S SIDE OF THE BED.

THE FOURTH WEEK GEORGE WAS AWAY, I FELL MADLY IN LOVE WITH HIM. I HATED MYSELF FOR MY WITHDRAWAL, FOR MY FAILURE OF HIM.

THE FIFTH WEEK GEORGE CAME HOME. THE MINUTE HE WALKED IN AND SAID: "I'M BACK, DARLING!" I WITHDREW.

I CAN HARDLY WAIT FOR HIS NEXT BUSI- NESS TRIP SO I CAN LOVE GEORGE AGAIN.

I MEET A GIRL. I TELL HER ALL OF MY MOST INTIMATE PERSONAL SECRETS WHICH SHE PROMISES NEVER TO REPEAT TO ANYBODY. THEN AFTER AWHILE WE BREAK UP.

I MEET ANOTHER GIRL. I TELL HER THINGS ABOUT ME I'VE NEVER REVEALED TO A SOUL WHICH SHE PROMISES NEVER TO REPEAT TO ANYBODY. A COUPLE OF MONTHS LATER WE ALWAYS BREAK UP.

THEN I MEET A NEW GIRL. I EXPOSE MY INNER-MOST FEELINGS TO HER IN A WAY I'VE NEVER QUITE DONE BEFORE— WHICH SHE PROMISES NEVER TO REVEAL TO ANYBODY. SOON IT ALL DIES BETWEEN US AND WE BREAK UP.

ALL OVER THE CITY GIRLS WHO NO LONGER LIKE ME ARE CASUALLY WALKING AROUND WITH MY LIFE'S CONFESSIONS—

EACH CARRYING AN INTIMATE PIECE OF ME— LETTING IT LOOSE TO GIRL FRIENDS—LETTING IT SLIP TO NEW BOY FRIENDS—SPREADING ME THIN AT PARTIES ALL OVER TOWN. THE **WORLD** KNOWS ABOUT BERNARD MERGENDIELER!

AND I'VE ALWAYS BEEN SO SECRETIVE.

EVER SINCE I WAS A LITTLE KID I DIDN'T WANT TO BE ME. I WANTED TO BE BILLIE WIDDLEDON. AND BILLIE WIDDLEDON DIDN'T EVEN **LIKE** ME.

I WALKED LIKE **HE** WALKED. I TALKED LIKE **HE** TALKED. I SIGNED UP FOR THE HIGH SCHOOL **HE** SIGNED UP FOR—

WHICH WAS WHEN BILLIE WIDDLEDON CHANGED. HE BEGAN TO HANG AROUND HERBY VANDEMAN. HE **WALKED** LIKE HERBY VANDEMAN. HE **TALKED** LIKE HERBY VANDEMAN.

HE MIXED ME UP! I BEGAN TO WALK AND TALK LIKE BILLIE WIDDLEDON WALKING AND TALKING LIKE HERBY VANDEMAN.

AND THEN IT DAWNED ON ME THAT HERBY VANDEMAN WALKED AND TALKED LIKE JOEY HAVERLIN AND JOEY HAVERLIN WALKED AND TALKED LIKE CORKY SABINSON.

SO HERE I AM WALKING AND TALKING LIKE BILLIE WIDDLEDON'S IMITATION OF HERBY VANDEMAN'S VERSION OF JOEY HAVERLIN TRYING TO WALK AND TALK LIKE CORKY SABINSON.

AND **WHO** DO YOU THINK CORKY SABINSON IS ALWAYS WALKING AND TALKING LIKE? OF **ALL** PEOPLE— DOPEY KENNY WELLINGTON—

THAT LITTLE PEST WHO WALKS AND TALKS LIKE ME.

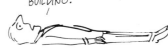

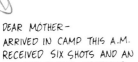

 WILLIE - COME OUT OF THERE! YOU'VE BEEN IN THERE LONG ENOUGH!

SOON MA. SOON -

 NOT SOON, WILLIE. **NOW!** WHAT ARE YOU DOING IN THERE ALL BY YOURSELF **ANY**HOW?

READING, MA. READING -

 YOUR FATHER DIDN'T GET A **BANK** LOAN TO BUILD **YOU** A **LIBRARY**, MISTER! YOU DO YOUR READING SOMEWHERE **ELSE** THAN HIS FALLOUT SHELTER!

IT'S **MY** FALLOUT SHELTER **TOO**, MA!

 **ARGUMENTS! ARGUMENTS!** YOU SAY IT'S YOURS - YOUR **SISTER** SAYS IT'S **HERS** - IT'S EVERYBODY'S FALLOUT SHELTER BUT MAMA'S!

YOU NEVER YELL AT SISTER WHEN **SHE'S** IN HERE.

 YOUR SISTER DUCKS EVERY TIME SHE HEARS A **PLANE!** YOU HAVE TO MAKE **ALLOWANCES** FOR YOUR SISTER!

I'LL BE OUT IN A MINUTE -

 WELL, CONGRATULATIONS, MISTER. YOU WEREN'T PLAYING WITH THE **MACHINE GUN** AGAIN WERE YOU?

HONEST, MA I WAS **READ**ING. I DIDN'T TOUCH **ANY**THING OF DAD'S.

 READING - READING - WHAT'S SO IMPORTANT THAT YOU WERE READING?

"YAHOO WORLD WAR III HOORAY COMICS."

 THE **THINGS** THEY'RE ATTRACTED TO! WHAT CAN YOU **DO** WITH KIDS TODAY?

 I DON'T KNOW WHAT'S THE MATTER WITH ME. I'M ALWAYS **READING.**

 MY MOTHER SAYS "LOOK AT LITTLE MISS KNOW-IT-ALL! HER NOSE IS ALWAYS IN A BOOK. YOU'LL NEVER CATCH A FELLA **THAT** WAY!"

 MY FATHER SAYS "WHAT DOES IT GET YOU TO BE A BOOK WORM? YOU'LL ONLY HURT YOUR EYES. YOU'LL FIND OUT WHEN YOU'RE OLDER THESE THINGS AREN'T SO IMPORTANT."

 MY TEACHER SAYS, "WELL, MISS BETTER-THAN-THE-REST-OF-US HAS **FINISHED** THE BOOK WHEN SHE WAS ONLY SUPPOSED TO READ UP TO **CHAPTER NINE**. PERHAPS THE REST OF US WHO **AREN'T** SHOW-OFFS CAN **STICK** TO OUR ASSIGNMENT."

 I **TRY** TO STOP, BUT IT GETS **WORSE** INSTEAD OF BETTER! I **READ!** I **READ!** I **READ!** NO MATTER **WHAT**, I CAN'T STOP READING!

 NEXT YEAR I GO TO HIGH SCHOOL.

 MAYBE **THEY** CAN HELP ME.

WHAT DO YOU THINK IS BETTER—THE '62 OR THE '63 "CORPUS"?

DAD HAD A '62, BUT THE CAM SHAFT KEPT LOSING FLUID, WHICH AFFECTED HIS TURNOVER REWIPE. RATHER THAN REORIENT, HE TRADED HER FOR A '61 "BREAKAGE."

MY DAD HAD A '62 "BREAKAGE" WHERE THEY FILED DOWN THE HEAD POINTS AND REWIRED THE VALVE SLAB IN ORDER TO DOUBLE THE GAS TAKE.

SURE, BUT THEN YOU HAVE TO COMPENSATE THE FRACTION-LOSS BY RERIGGING THE OIL JAM. AND **THAT** ALMOST ALWAYS LEADS TO FLOTSAM SLIPPAGE. I DON'T RECOMMEND IT.

WHAT **I'D** LOVE TO DRIVE IS THE "AMBULATORY 8." LIKE PEOPLE SAY, IT'S A LEMON, BUT IF YOU SHORTEN THE QUARTER RODS AND VALE BALANCE THE HOOPS YOU CAN — TOTALLY ELIMINATE SKIM!

NO KIDDING? I NEVER KNEW YOU COULD CORRECT FOR SKIM.

WELL, MORT, THAT'S WHAT SCHOOLS FOR. YOU LEARN SOMETHING EVERY DAY.

WILL THE CLASS PLEASE COME TO ORDER.

MORTON, WILL YOU PLEASE READ TODAY'S ENGLISH ASSIGNMENT?

"LOOK-AT-DICK. DICK-HAS-THEE-BALL. TOM-WANTS-THEE-BALL. RUN-DICK-RUN."

SO ONE DAY DADDY AND MOMMY ASKED ME— "WHAT DO YOU WANT TO BE WHEN YOU GROW UP, JOEY?" AND I SAID "A **COWBOY**."

SO DADDY SAID TO MOMMY, "HE'S A LITTLE OLD TO BEGIN, SO WE'LL HAVE TO APPLY RIGHT AWAY." AND HE TOOK ME TO THIS FUNNY KIND OF SCHOOL THAT GAVE ME A WHOLE LOT OF TESTS.

AND AFTER THE TESTS THE TEACHER TOLD DADDY, "THE TESTS PROVE THAT JOEY HAS THE **APTITUDE** TO BE A COWBOY, THE **MENTAL ALERTNESS** TO BE A COWBOY AND THE **CAREER INTEREST** TO BE A COWBOY. OF COURSE, HE'LL HAVE TO TAKE AN **EMOTIONAL QUALIFICATION** EXAM."

SO THEY GAVE ME ONE. AND AFTER THE TEST THE DOCTOR SAID TO DADDY, "THE TEST PROVES THAT JOEY WOULD MAKE AN EXCELLENT ADJUSTMENT TO THE WEST."

SO DADDY TOOK ME HOME AND SAID TO MOMMY— "WE'LL GET HIM INTO EXETER AND THEN INTO HARVARD AND THEN HE CAN TAKE HIS GRADUATE WORK IN COWBOY AT EITHER STANFORD OR U.C.L.A. DOESN'T THAT MAKE YOU HAPPY, JOEY?" AND I BEGAN TO CRY. AND MOMMY SAID, "WHAT'S THE MATTER, JOEY?"

AND I SAID, "I CHANGED MY MIND. I WANT TO BE A NURSE."

YOU SEE WHAT THE PROBLEM **IS**, A LOT OF THESE **NEW** COUNTRIES ARE COLORED AND THEY'RE— YOU **KNOW**— VERY OVER SENSITIVE.

BOY, DON'T I **KNOW!** YOU SHOULD SPEAK TO THE GIRL I HAVE COME IN ON MONDAYS.

AND I DON'T HAVE TO TELL YOU THE WAY IT IS— THEY DON'T HAVE OUR WEALTH OF **EXPERIENCE**— I MEAN BASICALLY THEY'RE A VERY **INNOCENT** PEOPLE— I MEAN— THEY'RE NOT SOPHISTICATED!

WELL, YOU'RE EITHER OR YOU'RE NOT I SAY.

THEN THEY COME TO THE UNITED NATIONS IN NEW YORK AND THEY EXPECT EVERYBODY TO BE THEIR **FRIEND**. THEY DON'T UNDERSTAND ABOUT NEW YORK. NOBODY'S **ANYBODY'S** FRIEND.

CAN YOU **IMAGINE**? THEY'RE VERY INNOCENT IF YOU ASK ME.

SO IF THEY GET TREATED NASTY IN A RESTAURANT OR FOR INSTANCE GET SHOVED IN THE STREET THEY THINK IT'S BECAUSE WE DON'T **RESPECT** THEM.

WELL I'VE DISCOVERED AFTER A LONG LIFE THAT YOU HAVE TO **EARN** RESPECT. IF YOU'RE NOT IN **TOO** MUCH OF A HURRY— IF YOU KNOW YOUR PL—

BUT YOU DON'T UNDERSTAND! DON'T YOU SEE THEY ALL HAVE CHIPS ON THEIR SHOULDER! SO NOW IT LOOKS LIKE IF WE DON'T SERVE THEM NICE IN OUR RESTAURANTS, THEY'LL ALL GO COMMUNIST.

COMMUNIST! AND I USED TO THINK THEY WERE ALL SO GOOD-NATURED. WELL YOU TURN YOUR BACK ON PEOPLE FOR A MINUTE AND—

SO RATHER THAN LET THEM GO COMMUNIST I SUPPOSE IT'S OUR DUTY TO HELP THEM— BUT AFTER ALL IT'S A HARD LIFE FOR **EVERYBODY**. I MYSELF DON'T ALWAYS GET THE BEST SERVICE IN RESTAURANTS. BUT **I'M** A GOOD SPORT. I LAUGH IT OFF.

AFRICA WOULD BE A LOT BETTER OFF IF IT WAS MORE LIKE YOU, DORIS.

WHEN A COUNTRY IS INVOLVED IN A LIFE AND DEATH STRUGGLE IT CAN'T BE ALL THAT LIBERALS WOULD **LIKE** IT TO BE.

THAT'S WHAT **MOST** PEOPLE DON'T **UNDERSTAND**- FOR INSTANCE, THE **PRESS**.

EXACTLY! ALL RIGHT, WHEN YOU'RE MORE OR LESS **SECURE** A PERFECTLY FREE PRESS THAT CAN PRINT ALL THE NEWS IS **FINE**

RIGHT! BUT IN A TIME OF **PERIL**, SOME INFORMATION **HAS** TO BE OVERLOOKED OR IT WOULD **CONFUSE** THE PEOPLE-

EXACTLY! AND ALL THIS TALK ABOUT **POLITICAL PRISONERS** -

CERTAINLY! WE **ALL** WANT TO BE **JUST**. BUT THE MOST **DANGEROUS** ENEMY IS THE ENEMY FROM **WITHIN!**

ABSOLUTELY! WHEN THE ENEMY IS ALL **AROUND** YOU **TRUE** DEMOCRACY JUST **ISN'T** ALWAYS **FEASIBLE!**

PRECISELY! AND **THAT'S** WHY I SAY OUR CRITICISM OF **CUBA** IS UNFAIR AND UNREALISTIC!

CUBA! I THOUGHT WE WERE TALKING ABOUT THE **UNITED STATES**-

WAITER

CHECK

DON'T GET ME WRONG- I THINK IT'S **WONDERFUL** THAT YOU KIDS ARE PROTESTING AGAIN. BUT WHY DON'T YOU PICKET THE **RUSSIANS**?

WE **ARE** PICKETING THE RUSSIANS.

DON'T GET ME WRONG- I **DEPLORE** THE APATHY THAT ONCE SWALLOWED OUR YOUTH, BUT AREN'T PICKET SIGNS THE CRUDEST FORM OF PUBLIC DEBATE?

WE'RE WILLING TO TALK.

DON'T GET ME WRONG - I **FAVOR** FULL DEBATE OF OUR GLOBAL POLICIES, BUT WON'T WE **HARM** OURSELVES BY SEEMING DIVIDED IN THE EYES OF THE REST OF THE WORLD?

THEN YOU'RE **AGAINST** PROTEST?

DON'T GET ME WRONG- I THINK IT'S **WONDERFUL** THAT YOU KIDS ARE PROTESTING AGAIN. BUT COULDN'T YOU FIND YOURSELVES **ANOTHER** FIELD?

WHAT WOULD YOU HAVE IN MIND?

I'LL ASK THE STATE DEPARTMENT TO DRAW UP SUGGESTIONS. IF WE CAN ONLY GET YOUTH TO JOIN IN **RESPONSIBLE** PROTEST IT CAN TEACH US **ALL** A VALUABLE LESSON -

DON'T GET ME WRONG-

NO SIR.

THE PRESIDENT DROPPED BY FOR BREAKFAST YESTERDAY. VERY UNEXPECTED.

WHY, OF COURSE. **YOUR** HOUSE IS ON THE WAY TO **MY** HOUSE. WE HAD LUNCH.

I TOLD HIM I WAS WRITING MY THURSDAY COLUMN ON EXECUTIVE POWER. I THINK ITS THE KEY TO **EVERYTHING!**

OH, IS **THAT** WHERE HE PICKED THAT UP? I SHOWED HIM MY FRIDAY COLUMN ON THE COMMON MARKET. **THAT'S** THE KEY TO EVERYTHING.

HE SEEMED TERRIBLY INTERESTED. HE SAID WE COULD DISCUSS IT FURTHER AT THE WHITE HOUSE RECEPTION FOR KATHERINE ANNE PORTER.

THE COMMON MARKET! THE ENTIRE FREE WORLD INCORPORATED INTO A TARIFF FREE EXCHANGE OF MISSILE WARHEADS! A NATO ALLIANCE FOR PROGRESS! I TOLD HIM!

POWER, I TOLD HIM. THE DEVIOUS INFLUENCE OF POWER! HE READ MY COLUMN WITH **AVID** INTEREST. EVEN FASTER THAN USUAL.

OF COURSE - HE ALWAYS SAYS TO ME - "JOE, NO MATTER HOW FAST I READ, YOU ALWAYS FINISH THE PAGE AHEAD OF ME."

"MR. PRESIDENT," I SAID (THOUGH I'VE KNOWN HIM FOR YEARS I STILL REFER TO HIM BY HIS CEREMONIAL TITLE), "IF I HAVE HELPED FORM POLICY IN ANY WAY - AS A NEWSPAPER MAN I'D RATHER NOT KNOW ABOUT IT." "WELL SAID, SCOTTY." HE REPLIED.

"JOE," HE LEAKED TO ME, "YOU'RE WORTH FIFTEEN DEAN RUSKS." "COME OFF IT, SIR," I ANSWERED, "I AM BUT A NEWSPAPERMAN."

I **AM** THE NEW FRONTIER.

NO, YOU'RE NOT! IT'S **ME!**

HOW DOES IT LOOK?

NOT TOO BAD, CHIEF. GALLUP HAS YOU DOWN 3% ON FISCAL RESPONSIBILITY, UP 2% ON GETTING TOUGH WITH LABOR, DOWN 4% ON GETTING TOUGH WITH BUSINESS.

HOW ABOUT ROPER?

ROPER HAS YOU UP 2% ON ATMOSPHERIC TESTING, DOWN 3% ON MEDICARE, UP 4% ON YOUR PHYSICAL FITNESS PROGRAM.

MMM - WHAT DOES HARRIS SAY?

HARRIS HAS YOU UP 2% ON OUR FAILURE TO REACH AGREEMENT AT GENEVA, UP 1% ON OUR FAILURE TO REACH AGREEMENT IN VIET NAM AND STANDING PAT ON CIVIL RIGHTS.

MMM - GOT THE TOTAL ON PRESS COMMENT?

YES SIR - THIS WEEK LIPPMANN WAS CAUTIOUS, RESTON HOPEFUL, ALSOP DISTURBED, LAWRENCE MOROSE, CHILDS WATCHFUL AND KEMPTON PAINED.

HOW POPULAR AM I?

MORE SO THAN LAST WEEK. LESS THAN THREE MONTHS AGO AT THIS TIME.

GET THOSE REPORTS OVER TO PLANNING AND HAVE THEM COORDINATED INTO A POPULAR POLICY. LET'S PUSH THOSE RATINGS UP!

IT'S TIME TO GET THIS COUNTRY MOVING AGAIN, EH, CHIEF?

THE RESUMPTION OF NUCLEAR TESTING ON THE PART OF ONE OF THE MAJOR POWERS POSES A DELICATE PROBLEM FOR SOME OF US IN THE NON-ALIGNED, UNCOMMITTED AND, IF YOU WILL, NEUTRAL NATIONS.

WE ARE ALL, OF COURSE, OPPOSED TO NUCLEAR TESTING BY ANYONE: FRANCE, BRITAIN, THE U.S., ISRAEL, **ANY**ONE.

BUT IN AN ATMOSPHERE OF PROVOCATION AND **COUNTER** PROVOCATION IT IS DIFFICULT TO POINT THE FINGER OF BLAME. SOME SAY IT IS THE FAULT OF **FRANCE** FOR HER SAHARA TESTING. SOME SAY IT IS THE **U.S.** FOR HER **OBVIOUS** PREPARATIONS TO **RESUME** TESTS. **SOME** EVEN BLAME THE SOVIET UNION.

WERE THE UNITED STATES TO HAVE RESUMED HER TESTING **FIRST** OUR PROBLEM WOULD HAVE BEEN A SIMPLER ONE. FOR **NOT** DOING SO WE MUST EXPRESS ADMIRATION FOR HER RESTRAINT AS WELL AS ANNOYANCE FOR OUR CURRENT DILEMMA.

ONE CANNOT OVERLOOK THAT WHILE THE RUSSIANS MAY WISH TO COLONIZE THE WEST, THE WEST HISTORICALLY HAS COLONIZED **US.** THIS MAY HAVE **SOME** BEARING ON THE FORM OF OUR MORAL OUTRAGE.

SO RATHER THAN CONDEMN ONE NATION AND THUS CONTRIBUTE TO WORLD TENSION WE FEEL IT WISER TO CONDEMN **BOTH**- THOSE WHO ARE TESTING AND THOSE WHO ARE NOT.

IT IS BEAUTIFUL TO BE IN BELGRADE NOW THAT AUTUMN'S HERE.

FOR TOO MANY YEARS, PROFESSOR, THE LAY PUBLIC HAS BEEN ILL INFORMED ON THE ISSUE OF NUCLEAR WAR. THEY HAVE BEEN **AGAINST** IT.

BECAUSE OF DELUSION, PROFESSOR. BECAUSE OF DELUSION.

NATURALLY. THEY THOUGHT ALL OF US WOULD BE **DESTROYED.** THIS CALLED FOR A MASSIVE ATTEMPT AT RE-EDUCATION WHICH I FEEL HAS BORNE FRUIT. THE LAY PUBLIC NO LONGER FEELS THAT ALL OF US WOULD BE DESTROYED.

QUITE TRUE, PROFESSOR. THE LAY PUBLIC NOW FEELS THAT ONLY **MOST** OF US WOULD BE DESTROYED.

HOPEFUL. NEVERTHELESS, PROFESSOR, THE LAY PUBLIC **STILL** DOES NOT ACCEPT THE FACTS AS WE **THEORISTS** PREFER TO BELIEVE THEM—

—THAT IN THE EVENT OF NUCLEAR WAR NO ONE NEED BE HURT AT ALL!

WELL REASONED, PROFESSOR. THE PROPER MOVE WOULD BE TO CONVINCE THE U.S.S.R. THAT WE WILL IGNORE **THEIR** POPULATION CENTERS IF THEY IGNORE **OURS.** IF WE CAN RESTRICT NUCLEAR WAR TO EACH OTHER'S MISSILE BASES IT MAY PROVE TO BE QUITE A CIVILIZED AFFAIR.

MUCH **NEATER** THAN RIVAL FORMS OF WAR, REALLY.

NO LOSS OF LIVES. ONLY MISSILE BASES. PRACTICALLY A DISARMAMENT PROGRAM, REALLY. I WOULD THINK IT SHOULD EVEN ENLIST THE SUPPORT OF THE **PACIFISTS** IN OUR MIDST!

AND WHAT A BOON TO FULL EMPLOYMENT! WE CAN JUST REBUILD AND START ALL OVER AGAIN!

HAPPY WARS, PROFESSOR.

LET'S ALL JOIN HANDS AND PUSH.

ONCE THERE WAS A RICH MERCHANT WHO HAD THREE HANDSOME YOUNG SONS TO WHOM HE ONE DAY PRESENTED A GIFT OF THREE BOWS AND THREE ARROWS.
"EACH OF YOU WILL SHOOT A SINGLE ARROW" INSTRUCTED THE FATHER "IN THE DIRECTION THAT YOUR ARROWS FLY THERE WILL YOU FIND YOUR FORTUNES."

THE ELDEST SON FOLLOWED HIS ARROW TO WASHINGTON, MARRIED A BEAUTIFUL PRINCESS AND BECAME A BELOVED RULER ADMIRED FOR THE MANNER IN WHICH HE SOUGHT WORLD PEACE AND SENT TROOPS TO ASIER.

THE MIDDLE BROTHER FOLLOWED **HIS** ARROW TO WASHINGTON, MARRIED A BEAUTIFUL PRINCESS AND BECAME A LEGAL SCHOLAR, A FRIEND OF MINORITIES AND AN ADVOCATE OF A WIRE TAP BILL.

THE YOUNGEST BROTHER MARRIED A BEAUTIFUL PRINCESS AND JUST HUNG AROUND FOR AWHILE. HE WAS TOO YOUNG TO PLAY WITH BOWS AND ARROWS. HIS OLDER BROTHERS CRIED "**COME TO WASHINGTON! COME TO WASHINGTON!**"
"BUT I CAN'T WORK THIS DARN THING!" SAID THE YOUNGER BROTHER STILL TOO UNCOORDINATED TO PUT THE ARROW TO THE BOW.

"WE CAN'T HELP YOU" SAID THE OLDER BROTHER PLACING THE ARROW IN HIS HAND.
"YOU MUST DO IT YOURSELF" SAID THE MIDDLE BROTHER PLACING THE BOW IN THE PROPER POSITION.
"IT'S UP TO YOU" SAID BOTH BROTHERS AS THEY SHOT THE BOW, THE ARROW AND THE YOUNGER BROTHER ALL THE WAY TO WASHINGTON.

MORAL: NO MATTER WHO YOU ARE IT'S NICE TO HAVE EVERYTHING.

DOES YOUR PARTY, THE **RADICAL MIDDLE**, HAVE ANY VIEWS ON EXTREMIST CANDIDATES RUNNING FOR PRESIDENT?

THE RADICAL MIDDLE ONLY SUPPORTS RADICAL MIDDLE CANDIDATES. HOWEVER SINCE **LIBERAL** PRESIDENTS INVARIABLY MOVE TO THE **RIGHT** AND **CONSERVATIVE** PRESIDENTS INVARIABLY MOVE TO THE **LEFT**, THE RADICAL MIDDLE WILL SUPPORT WHOMEVER WINS.

THEREFORE, YOU TAKE NO POSITION, SAY, IN THE CURRENT FIGHT FOR THE REPUBLICAN NOMINATION?

WHILE IT IS TRUE THAT GOVERNOR ROCKEFELLER WAS A PREMATURE RADICAL MIDDLER WE SEE SIGNS OF SENATOR GOLDWATER'S BECOMING A **LATENT** RADICAL MIDDLER. THUS IN **OUR** VIEW THERE IS NO IMPORTANT DIFFERENCE BETWEEN THEM.

WOULDN'T YOU CALL THAT A SURPRISING STATEMENT IN VIEW OF THEIR STATED POLICY DIFFERENCES?

THE RADICAL MIDDLE BELIEVES THAT ALL POWER, ONCE OBTAINED, COLLAPSES TOWARD THE MIDDLE. IT LITTLE MATTERS WHAT ANYONE SAYS HE STANDS FOR.

AREN'T YOU BEING UNDULY CYNICAL?

ON THE CONTRARY. **WE** ADVOCATE JUST SUCH A COLLAPSE TOWARD THE MIDDLE. OUR MOTTO: "THAT GOVERNMENT IS BEST WHICH COLLAPSES MOST."

BUT IF ALL WHO WIN POWER COLLAPSE TO THE SAME POSITION, WHAT'S THE POINT OF ELECTING **ANYONE**?

THE RADICAL MIDDLE STRONGLY FAVORS FREE ELECTIONS JUST SO LONG AS THERE CONTINUE TO BE NO REAL DIFFERENCES BETWEEN THE PARTIES. THEY SERVE AS AN INTERESTING TRIBAL RITE AND MAKE **MARVELOUS** PROPAGANDA VALUE.

THEN YOU HAVE NO PREFERENCE AT ALL IN NEXT YEAR'S ELECTIONS?

WE HAVE MET THE CANDIDATES AND THEY ARE OURS.

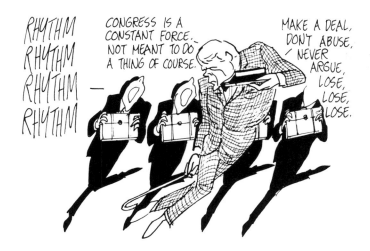

FOR A SOCIETY—**ANY** SOCIETY—TO FUNCTION PROPERLY IT NEEDS **OUTLETS-RELEASES.** IT NEEDS **ENTERTAINMENT** AND **DIVERTING TRIVIA.** IN OUR SOCIETY FOR ENTERTAINMENT WE HAVE **THEATRE,** WE HAVE **MOVIES,** WE HAVE **TV.**

FOR DIVERTING TRIVIA WE HAVE A FREE PRESS.

THE FUNCTION OF A FREE PRESS, AS WE KNOW IT, IS NOT TO PUBLISH **ALL** THE NEWS. WHO'D **READ** IT? IT'S NOT EVEN TO PUBLISH THE TRUTH. WHO'D **KNOW** IT? THE FUNCTION OF A FREE PRESS IS TO PUBLISH FREE PRESS RELEASES.

THUS IF A RELIABLE PENTAGON SOURCE LEAKS AN ANTI-DISARMAMENT STORY ALL THE ANTI-DISARMAMENT PRESS WILL PLAY IT UP **BIG** WHILE THE **PRO**-DISARMAMENT PRESS (WHAT THERE IS OF IT) WILL BURY IT ON PAGE FORTY.

OR IF A RELIABLE JUSTICE DEPARTMENT SOURCE LEAKS A PRESS RELEASE ON SOME NEW **ANTI-MONOPOLY** PROSECUTION, THE ANTI-MONOPOLY PRESS (WHAT THERE IS OF IT) WILL PLAY IT UP BIG WHILE THE **PRO-** MONOPOLY PRESS WILL BURY IT ON PAGE FORTY TILL THEY CAN TIE IT TO A PRESS RELEASE ON THE NEXT **JIMMY HOFFA** PROSECUTION.

IF A CRITIC OF THE STATE IS JAILED BEHIND THE IRON CURTAIN OUR PRESS WILL PUBLISH SELF-RIGHTEOUS EDITORIALS DENOUNCING ALL POLITICAL PERSECUTION. IF A CRITIC OF A CONGRESSIONAL COMMITTEE IS JAILED **OVER HERE** OUR PRESS WILL PUBLISH SELF RIGHTEOUS EDITORIALS PROCLAIMING THAT FREE SPEECH DOESN'T GIVE ANYONE THE RIGHT TO CRY "FIRE" IN A CROWDED THEATRE.

EVERY PAPER HAS ITS OWN **LINE** AND STICKS TO IT. EVERY PAPER HAS ITS OWN PROSPECTUS—"ALL THE NEWS THAT'S SAFE TO PRINT"—AND IT STICKS TO **THAT.**

FREE PRESS? WE'RE A NATION OF TRADE JOURNALS.

WHO WAS AT THE BUDGET HEARING? ANYBODY GOT THE STORY?

I GOT IT. I STOPPED BY ON MY WAY TO THE BARBER SHOP. HERE'S THE PRESS RELEASE THEY WERE HANDING OUT.

THANKS, GUS. WAIT A MINUTE AND I'LL GIVE YOU MY HANDOUT FROM THE A.E.C.

YEAH. I NEED THAT.

WHO'S GOT INTERNAL SECURITY? I **NEED** INTERNAL SECURITY!

I GOT IT. WHAT'VE YOU GOT FOR ME?

WHAT DO YOU NEED? I JUST PICKED UP TODAY'S PENTAGON FROM A GUY FROM REUTERS.

HEY, ANYBODY HERE HAVE FOREIGN RELATIONS?

I HAVE FOREIGN RELATIONS, BUT YOU STILL OWE ME FROM YESTERDAY WHEN I GAVE YOU SENATE JUDICIARY.

I'LL MAKE A DEAL. I'LL GIVE YOU **MY** WAYS AND MEANS AND RIVERS AND HARBORS FOR **YOUR** FOREIGN RELATIONS.

WELL, FAIR'S FAIR. NOW ALL I NEED IS A WHITE HOUSE PRESS RELEASE.

I'LL PICK IT UP, GUS. I HAVE TO STOP BY FOR A PRESS RELEASE ON NEWS MANAGEMENT. ANYBODY NEED ANYTHING ELSE?

YEAH. BRING ME BACK A HAM ON RYE.

THE WHITE HOUSE, NEWS MANAGEMENT AND A HAM ON RYE. HEY, WHO KNOWS A GOOD LUNCHEONETTE AROUND HERE?

I'VE NEVER BEEN ABLE TO FIND ONE. LET'S WAIT FOR A PRESS RELEASE.

I FOUND
A FLOWER!

I FOUND
A
FLOWER!

MY FLOWER IS BIG
AND BEAUTIFUL AND
EXTREMELY ROBUST.

THAT'S
TRUE.

YOUR FLOWER
IS DARK AND
UNGAINLY AND
MAY NOT LIVE
TILL MORNING.

IT WILL
CERTAINLY
BE A
STRUGGLE.

I **LOVE** MY FLOWER FOR ALL
ITS RICHNESS AND GRANDEUR.

I LOVE MY
FLOWER FOR
ITS SPIRITUAL
VALUES.

WHAT
SPIRITUAL
VALUES?

MY FLOWER
IS A TRAGIC
FLOWER. IT
HAS SOUL.
IT HAS
POETRY.

JUST BECAUSE
MY FLOWER
IS BIGGER
IT CAN'T
HAVE
POETRY?

MY FLOWER MUST
STRUGGLE FOR
HOURLY SURVIVAL.
IT IS TAKEN WITH
BASICS. IT BROODS
ABOUT THE
DEEP
THINGS.

ARE YOU CALLING
MY FLOWER A
DILETTANTE?

YOUR FLOWER
IS RICH AND
PROBABLY HAS
A LEISURE
PROBLEM.

I SUDDENLY FEEL LIKE
BEATING YOUR FLOWER
OVER THE HEAD WITH
MY FLOWER.

MY
FLOWER
WOULD
DIE-
LOVINGLY.

I APOLOGIZE.
I HAVE A
VULGAR FLOWER.

MY FLOWER
TRULY
UNDERSTANDS.

WITH US TONIGHT TO GIVE HIS VIEWS ON THE CURRENT RACIAL CRISIS, IS A SPOKESMAN FOR THAT GROUP WE HEAR MORE AND MORE FROM THESE DAYS— THE **RADICAL MIDDLE**.

VERY SERIOUS. EXTREMELY GRAVE. DEEPLY DISTURBING.

AS I UNDERSTAND YOUR GROUP, SIR, IT ADVOCATES AN IRRESPONSIBLE MIDDLE POSITION. IS THAT CORRECT?

YES AND NO. FOR INSTANCE IN THE FIELD OF LABOR WE HAVE TRADITIONALLY RECOGNIZED THE RIGHT TO ORGANIZE WHILE BEING TRADITIONALLY CRITICAL OF THE NEED TO STRIKE.

OR, IN THE FIELD OF CIVIL LIBERTIES— WE HAVE TRADITIONALLY FAVORED THE BILL OF RIGHTS WHILE BEING TRADITIONALLY CRITICAL OF ITS ACROSS-THE-BOARD IMPLEMENTATION.

AND SO, TODAY IN THE FIELD OF CIVIL RIGHTS. WE TRADITIONALLY RECOGNIZE THE NEGROES' RIGHT TO PROTEST WHILE BEING TRADITIONALLY OPPOSED TO LEGISLATIVE CONCESSIONS WON BY PUBLIC DEMAND.

THEN SIR, YOUR ADVICE WOULD BE—

CONCILIATION. RESPONSIBLE MODERATES FROM BOTH SIDES SHOULD MEET AND MEET AND MEET UNTIL THEY NAIL DOWN FIRM PROPOSALS ON WHICH ALL MEN OF GOOD WILL CAN UNANIMOUSLY AGREE.

BUT, SIR, WON'T THAT TAKE **YEARS**?

I CAN WAIT.

BILLIE CAME OVER TO ME IN THE MORNING AND SAID YOU PROMISED TO TAKE ME TO THE ZOO TODAY, DADDY. AND I SAID I'M SORRY BILLIE-BOY BUT DADDY HAS GOT SOMETHING ELSE HE MUST DO TODAY.

AND BILLIE'S MOMMA SAID NOW YOU STOP BOTHERING YOUR DADDY, BILLIE-BOY. AND I SAID DON'T SCOLD THE BOY, CHARLOTTE. I KNOW JUST THE WAY HE FEELS BECAUSE I STILL REMEMBER WHAT IT WAS LIKE WHEN **MY** DADDY DISAPPOINTED **ME**.

AND CHARLOTTE HUGGED ME AND CALLED ME HER HONEY-BEAR AND SAID YOU'RE TOO GENTLE FOR YOUR OWN GOOD, DANNY. AND I SAID IT'S A BAD THING WHEN A FATHER HAS TO BREAK A PROMISE TO HIS SON. THAT'S THE WAY A CHILD CAN TURN SOUR.

AND CHARLOTTE SAID NO CHILD OF OURS WILL TURN SOUR SO LONG AS A MAN LIKE YOU IS AROUND. AND I HUGGED HER AND SAID YOU'RE MY LITTLE GIRL. THEN I PICKED UP MY BAT AND I SAID I'D BEST BE ON MY WAY. I'M LATE AS IT IS.

HIT ONE FOR ME, CHARLOTTE YELLED. AND FOR ME TOO, DADDY, BILLIE-BOY YELLED. AND I YELLED BACK DON'T YOU WORRY ABOUT ME. I'LL DO FINE.

AND THEN I DROVE DOWN-TOWN TO THE CIVIL RIGHTS DEMONSTRATIC

YOU'RE UNDER ARREST. COME ALONG, QUIETLY.

I KNOW MY RIGHTS. YOU'RE NOT A POLICEMAN. ONLY A POLICEMAN CAN ARREST ME.

THERE **ARE** NO MORE POLICEMEN. ONLY POLICE DOGS. WE'VE ELIMINATED THE MIDDLE MAN. COME ALONG, QUIETLY.

I KNOW MY RIGHTS. I'LL CALL THE F.B.I.

THE F.B.I. WORKS HAND IN PAW WITH LOCAL LAW ENFORCEMENT DOGS. COME ALONG, QUIETLY.

I KNOW MY RIGHTS. I'LL GO THROUGH THE COURTS.

THE COURTS TAKE **FOREVER**. WHY ELSE WOULD WE ENCOURAGE YOU TO USE THEM? COME ALONG, QUIETLY.

I KNOW MY RIGHTS. I'LL PICKET NON-VIOLENTLY.

NON-VIOLENCE MAY MAKE US FEEL GUILTY BUT WE CAN LEARN TO LIVE WITH IT. COME ALONG QU—HEY-WHAT DO YOU THINK **YOU'RE** DOING?

WHAT DOES IT **LOOK** LIKE I'M DOING?

TELL ME-WHAT IS IT YOU PEOPLE WANT?

LET ME PUT IT DIS WAY. WE HAD WOT WE CALLED "MEMBUHS."

WHAT'S THAT AGAIN? "MEMBUHS"?

'ATS RIGHT. AND THE "MEMBUHS" WAS DIVIDED INTO WOT WE CALLED "POTTIES."

HOW MANY OF THESE "POTTIES" WERE THERE?

DERE WAS ON'Y TWO "POTTIES." D'"DEMO-CRATIC POTTY" AND D' "REPUB-LICAN POTTY."

NOW THESE "POTTIES"- HOW DID THEY GET ALONG?

WELL, DEY WAS ALWEEZ, Y'KNOW, AT **WAR** WID EACH UDDER BUT IT NEVER **MEANT** ANYTING. I MEAN WHENEVER DERE WAS A **REAL** THREAT-LIKE FROM "D' **PEEPUL**" DEY'D BAND TOGEDDER AND FIGHT 'EM OFF.

"D'PEEPUL"? WHO WERE "D'PEEPUL"?

"D'PEEPUL"? WELL LET ME PUT IT DIS WAY. D'HIGHEST LEVEL WE CALLED "D'**SENATE**." D'LEVEL UNDER DAT WE CALLED "D'**HOUSE**." D'BOTTOM LEVEL WE CALLED "D'-**PEEPUL**." WE'D ON'Y USE DEM TO TAKE ADVAN'AGE AND GET MONEY.

BUT DID **NOONE** PROTEST THIS SHOCKING CONSPIRACY?

NO SUH. WE'D DI-VERT DERE ATTENTION.

HOW?

WE'D INVESTIGATE CRIME.

I HAVE COMPLETED MY FACT FINDING MISSION TO THE U.S. AND THESE ARE MY CONCLUSIONS.

I.- THE U.S. ADMINISTRATION IS TAKING AN INCREASINGLY SOFT LINE TOWARD THE COMMUNIST CONSPIRACY AND MAY HAVE TO BE IMPRISONED.

II.- THE U.S. CONGRESS IS EMBROILED IN QUERULOUS AND TIME WASTING DEBATE ON INTERNAL AFFAIRS AND MAY HAVE TO BE IMPRISONED.

III.- THE U.S. CLERGY ENGAGES IN "FREEDOM" RIDES FOR DIVISIVE ETHICAL PURPOSES. THEY MAY HAVE TO BE IMPRISONED.

WHILE YOUR C.I.A. AND YOUR F.B.I. HAVE MANY HEALTHY ATTITUDES THEIR LEADERSHIP HAS BECOME TOO OLD TO BE EFFECTIVELY UNLEASHED. THEY MAY HAVE TO BE IMPRISONED.

V.- THE AMERICAN PRESS CONTINUES TO BE SADLY MISINFORMED ON ASIAN AFFAIRS. IT MAY HAVE TO BE IMPRISONED.

IT IS **MY** OPINION THAT THE IMMEDIATE INSTITUTION OF THESE REFORMS WILL GO A LONG WAY TO IMPROVING THE STRAINED RELATIONS BETWEEN OUR TWO COUNTRIES.

YOU ARE ALL UNDER ARREST.

ONCE THERE WAS A SLEEPING COUNTRY THAT HAD SPENT EIGHT YEARS UNDER A SPELL. NOBODY TALKED. NOBODY ARGUED. EVERYBODY SLEPT.

THEN ONE DAY INTO THIS COUNTRY RODE A HANDSOME YOUNG PRINCE. "IT'S TIME TO GET MOVING AGAIN," THE PRINCE DECLARED. THE COUNTRY STIRRED IN ITS SLEEP.

FOR THE FIRST TIME IN YEARS PEOPLE ACTUALLY BEGAN TO **TALK**. THEY **ARGUED**. THEY **TOOK SIDES**. "STOP TALKING SO LOUD!" THE REST OF THE COUNTRY GRUMBLED IN ITS SLEEP. "HAVE SOME CONSIDERATION FOR THE REST OF US."

BUT THE TALKING ONLY BECAME LOUDER. MORE AND MORE PEOPLE AWOKE AND, ANGRY THAT THEY HAD TO BE AWAKE, BEGAN TO **TALK**, BEGAN TO **ARGUE**, BEGAN TO **TAKE SIDES**.

THEN ONE DAY THE YOUNG PRINCE WAS KILLED- NO ONE COULD AGREE BY WHOM. EVERY SIDE ACCUSED EVERY OTHER SIDE. BUT CALMER HEADS PREVAILED.

"SEE WHAT WE HAVE COME TO WITH THIS WICKED DISSENSION," CALMER HEADS ARGUED, "LET US CLEANSE OUR SOCIETY OF THIS DIVISIVE DEBATE!"

AND THE COUNTRY, SUFFERING FROM WOUNDS AND GUILT, **CHEERED**. DEBATE HALTED. ARGUMENT DIED. AND THERE WAS NO MORE TALK IN THE LAND.

AND AS THE COUNTRY PREPARED FOR SLEEP IT HOPED NO ONE WOULD EVER ASK IT TO MOVE AGAIN—

FOR IT REALLY DID NOT WANT TO KILL ANYMORE PRINCES.

SO YOU SEE, DEAR BERNARD, WHILE I THINK YOU'RE SWEET AND KIND AND GOOD— I CAN NEVER LOVE YOU.

SMACK

BERNARD, YOU HIT ME.

YES I DID! WANT TO SEE ME DO IT AGAIN?

BUT BERNARD, THAT SO UNLIKE YOU. YOU'RE NOT VIOLENT!

NO, I'M NOT VIOLENT AND WHERE HAS IT GOTTEN ME? IT'S GOTTEN ME TO BE SWEET, KIND AND GOOD! WANT TO GET HIT AGAIN?

BUT WHAT'S WRONG WITH BEING SWEET, KIND AND GOOD?

I'LL TELL YOU WHAT'S WRONG—I'M BEING SWALLOWED ALIVE! I'M THE SLAVE OF MY SWEETNESS, MY KINDNESS AND MY GOODNESS! BOY, DO I FEEL LIKE SMACKING YOU!

BUT WHAT DOES HITTING SOLVE?

WHAT DOES SOLVING SOLVE? NOTHING SOLVES NOTHING SO WHAT'S WRONG WITH HITTING! THAT'S MY PHILOSOPHY. STAND STILL—I THINK I'LL PUNCH YOU—

I WARN YOU, BUSTER—YOU LAY A HAND ON ME, I'LL KNOCK YOUR TEETH OUT.

VIOLENCE. SOMEHOW I FEEL CLEANER THAN I HAVE IN MONTHS.

VIOLENCE. HOW MUCH BETTER THAN HURTING YOU WITH WORDS.

OUTHOUISE DOOR

FILM STRIP 20"+ 20" BY DOUG SLADE

HARVARD PUBLIC LIBRARY

STARTING 1.20.2020

4 POND ROAD ♥ IN THE BROWSING ROOM

HERE LIES LYNDON

After the assassination of John F. Kennedy, I remember saying to friends: "He didn't accomplish much and he won't be remembered."

However, even I was aware that, overnight, American life had become terribly fragile. If a buoyant, powerful, energetic president could so easily be blown away, then who was safe? Certainly not I. Kennedy, for all my contempt, represented a new, hopeful spirit out there. He represented youthfulness. And hair. What hair! I couldn't help comparing it to my own baldness. If a bullet could cut through that shieldlike mane, what chance did I have?

It was as if any shot from any window in any direction could kill a president, as if history could be voted out of office by one madman—no more cycles, no more tides, no more critical analysis to understand the meaning of it all.

Kennedy's murder was intensely depressing. Oswald's murder converted the experience into farce. This was not a serious country anymore. This was not a place with meaning. A screw had come loose.

I can't live in that context. People need meaning. That's why we created religion, science, sociology and conspiracy theories. We demand a running order. Mine, for Kennedy's death, was the Cold War. The gray, ghastly Eisenhower-McCarthy years, the penting up of our national will had set off seismic disturbances of the spirit, muffled blasts of thwarted hope. Kennedy raised hope back to the surface. The distance between promise and fulfillment was no longer to be tolerated. Something had to go. I suspected Kennedy and Oswald were only the beginning, that a wave of irrational violence was going to take over the society, random acts with no apparent political content—but quite political in that they symbolized our dementia.

Kennedy's successor noted the dementia, hunkered down and took its measure, outfoxed it with a breathtaking end run of domestic reform, and then, just when he had it bloodied, turned tail and surrendered foreign policy to it. Within three years of taking office, Lyndon Johnson all but succeeded in turning Vietnam into a parking lot and America into a war zone. Protesters outside the White House gate chanted: "Hey, hey, LBJ, how many kids did you kill today?" Addressed to anyone but Johnson, the question might have been cruel.

LBJ was not only the First Man, he had turned into the first bully, the first liar, the first thief, the first credibility gap, the first war criminal, the first crack in the system, the first reason to riot in the streets, the first terrorist to the American Dream. The country has yet to survive him.

But mine is the rage of a lover betrayed. I don't often trust public figures; Johnson seduced me. In the nine months following Kennedy's assassination, his actions were extraordinary. I thought he was the best president since FDR.

In his early days in office, he was perceived as a Rooseveltian figure, a brilliant political strategist, the nation's number one civil rights leader, a man touched so by his own childhood poverty that he intended to see all poverty wiped out in his lifetime.

He employed his mythic deal-making and leadership skills to pass the kind of legislation he had buried in the Senate during his years as Majority Leader: The Voting Rights Act, The War on Poverty, Medicare....He behaved like a reformed gangster; he had the faith. Kennedy had only brought fashion back into fashion, Johnson brought social justice.

He was so good he was lousy to draw. An overabundance of oversized features made caricature difficult, made friendly caricature damned near impossible. It was beyond ordinary talent to do a drawing of Johnson that looked like Johnson and, at the same time, made him look honest. However well disposed one was to the president, his eyes were cold and nasty and the set of his mouth bore an unfortunate resemblance to that of the man at the bank who turns down your loan.

Anyhow, I liked Johnson. I can't draw a president I like. As a political satirist, my pen only works where it can hurt. So Johnson was good for the country but killing my business. Until he started bombing North Vietnam.

Defenders of the president claimed that what his critics really had against him was his style, but style only became a problem after he won as a peace candidate and promptly went to war. Before the policy of escalation, we didn't know who the president really was. Then we found out. We came to see him as not vital but violent, not clever but devious, not shrewd but cynical, not political but hypocritical, not populist but paranoiac.

While there were serious moral objections to Lyndon Johnson's involvement in Vietnam, these mainly troubled the peace movement. The issue that troubled the American people was that we were not winning. Johnson had dropped more bombs per month on North Vietnam than were dropped per month on Europe and Africa in World War II, and we were not winning. He had sent a half million American troops to join over 600,000 South Vietnamese troops, and we were not winning.

Here we had the first war in history to have its news coverage entirely in color, and we were not winning! Small reason bitterness swept the land. Americans are winners. We had never lost a war. So it was not Vietnam, but the fact that he was not winning in Vietnam that made Americans look more critically upon Lyndon Johnson. Winning was the trait that first recommended him to our favor: If we were to love him at all, it had to be for that. There was little else to admire him for. Joe McCarthy had more charm, Richard Nixon more sincerity. As Joseph Alsop put it, "The fact had to be faced that President Johnson has an uninspiring, perhaps even a downright bad moral style."

Late in his administration, Johnson commissioned the painter Peter Hurd to do his portrait. His comment on the finished painting was: "That's the ugliest thing I ever saw." An apt comment on Johnson's work, not Hurd's.

In the Johnson years, belief in law and, beyond that, belief in a polity known as the United States of America seemed on the point of collapse. To growing numbers, government ceased to have meaning except as a repressive and ineffectual policing mechanism. Non-violence was written off as *irrelevant*, a favorite word of the time. On television, we watched violence by blacks burning down their ghettos, we watched violence by anti-war whites trashing "Amerika." On the West Coast, left-wing and right-wing families bought guns for self-defense in the upcoming revolution.

Communication was out, co-opted by the Establishment. The drug culture was in. Getting high, getting down, getting my act together, getting my shit together, get off my case, don't lay a number on me, don't lay your trip on me, I'm cool, I'm hip, I'm wiped out, that blows me away, I want to do my thing, let's rap, we had a good rap, good dope, good grass, good hash, good speed, good acid, good smack, open the jails, the streets belong to the people, power to the people, oh wow.

Jerry Rubin, the Yippie, said, "You can't trust anyone over 30." He also said, "Shoot your father and mother." Students for a Democratic Society ran through high schools banging on doors, screaming into classrooms, "Jail break!"

Bob Dylan sang, "Something is happening here and you don't know what it is, do you, Mr. Jones?" Eldridge Cleaver wrote, "If you're not part of the solution, you're part of the problem." Smugness passed for revolution.

Bernard Mergendeiler did not take a view on the war, but he kept up with the times: he turned violent. In small ways, small acts, fantasies. He said and did mean things openly—almost openly, on occasion, admitting in his way, more or less, hostility, sort of, toward women. Ploddingly, he made clear that the dream of the comic little man was not, as Thurber had it in Walter Mitty, a dream of grandeur. Beneath the grandeur was a dream of getting even.

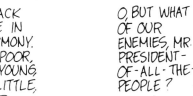

AS YOUR
PRESENT
PRESIDENT —
IT IS
INCUMBENT
UPON ME
TO PLAY
A VARIETY
OF ROLES
IN THE
COURSE
OF A
SINGLE
DAY.

POLICEMAN
TO THE —
WORLD.

SOCIAL
WORKER —
TO THE
POOR.

LOVER
OF
PEACE. —

SEEKER
OF CON-
SENSUS.

EDUCATOR. —

CIVIL RIGHTS
LEADER. —

AT THE
CLOSE
OF DAY —
WHAT A
RELIEF
IT IS TO
BE ABLE
TO GIT
IN MY
PAJAMAS —

AND
JUST —
BE
MYSELF.

IF EVER I THINK I'M FINALLY **MATURE-**

 I'LL GIVE MY-SELF THE **ACID TEST.**

 I'LL GO VISIT MY PARENTS.

 AND MY MOTHER WILL TELL ME I'VE LOST WEIGHT AND DON'T LOOK HAPPY.

 AND MY FATHER WILL TELL ME I SHOULDN'T BE SUCH A SMART GUY AND WHY DON'T I GIVE MORE MONEY HOME?

 AND MY MOTHER WILL ASK ME WHY I'M NOT EATING AND ISN'T HER COOKING GOOD ENOUGH FOR ME?

 AND MY FA-THER WILL TELL ME A STORY I'VE HEARD 500 TIMES BEFORE AND ASK IF HE'S **BORING** ME.

 AND BOTH OF THEM WILL ASK WHY THEY DON'T SEE ME MORE OFTEN.

 AND IF I CAN GET THROUGH THAT WHOLE EVENING WITHOUT FEELING AS IF I'M TEN YEARS OLD-

 I'M A **MAN!**

IT'S NOT GROWING.

OF COURSE NOT. IT'S WINTER.

BUT I GIVE IT **LOVE.** ALWAYS BEFORE WHEN I GAVE IT LOVE IT **GREW** IN WINTER.

APPARENTLY IT GOT **USED** TO LOVE. NOW IT DEMANDS SOME-THING ELSE TO GROW IN WINTER.

BUT WHAT ELSE CAN I GIVE IT? I GIVE IT WATER. I GIVE IT PLANT FOOD. I GIVE IT LOVE. - WHAT ELSE IS THERE TO GIVE?

HAVE YOU TRIED MONEY?

MY FLOWER WOULD NOT ACCEPT MONEY!

IT'S ONLY A SUGGESTION. OF COURSE IF YOU'RE AFRAID TO SEE WHAT WOULD **HAPPEN-**

I AM **NOT** AFRAID. I **KNOW** WHAT WOULD HAPPEN. LOOK, FLOWER- HERE'S FIVE DOLLARS! IT'S GROW-ING!

HERE'S **TEN** DOLLARS! LOOK AT IT GROW!

HERE'S ONE HUNDRED DOLLARS! GOOD HEAVENS, IT'S A TREE!

CONGRATULATIONS. YOUR FLOWER HAS AN EXCELLENT MIND FOR BUSINESS. MY FLOWER'S A SELL-OUT.

 I DON'T UNDER-STAND HOW IT HAPPENED BUT WHEN I WOKE UP YESTERDAY MORNING – I **KNEW** SOMETHING HAD CHANGED!

 I DIDN'T LOOK LIKE **ME** ANY-MORE! I LOOKED LIKE CARY GRANT.

 I LOOKED IN THE MIRROR AND SURE ENOUGH – THERE IT WAS – CARY GRANT.

 I LOOKED IN THE MIRROR AND SURE ENOUGH – THERE IT WAS – CARY GRANT.

 I WALKED DOWN THE STREET AND I COULD SEE IT IN THE WAY PEOPLE STARED AT ME – CARY GRANT.

I WENT TO THE OF-FICE AND EVERYBODY SEEMED **SHY** IN MY PRESENCE. GIRLS STARTED HANGING AROUND MY DESK. **MY DESK.** THE BOSS OFFERED ME A JOB IN THE PARIS OFFICE. CARY GRANT.

 I CALLED UP THE MOST BEAUTIFUL GIRL I KNEW. SHE SAID SHE HAD A DATE BUT SHE'D BREAK IT. SHE SAID SHE'D PICK UP TICKETS TO THE THEATER. CARY GRANT.

 WE WENT DANCING AFTER THE THEATER. I DIDN'T EVEN KNOW I KNEW **HOW!** PEOPLE FORMED A CIRCLE AROUND US AND APPLAUDED.

 I WENT HOME FLOATING. I WENT TO SLEEP DREAMING. THIS MORN-ING I WOKE UP AND KNEW SOME-THING HAD CHANGED.

 BACK TO BERNARD MERGEN-DEILER.

FOR PLAIN PEOPLE THERE IS NO SUCH THING AS A PERM-ANENT CARY GRANT.

 "AND NOW, THE FINAL CHAPTER IN TONIGHT'S SHOW." "LADIES AND GENTLE MEN!"

 "I'VE JUST LEARNED WE HAVE SOME-ONE VERY SPECIAL IN OUR AUDI-ENCE – **MR. BERNARD MERG-ENDEILER!** PERHAPS WE CAN COAX HIM UP HERE TO FAVOR US WITH ONE OF HIS IMMORTAL SONGS AND TAP DANCES!" "WELL, GEE.." YAY! PHWEET! BERNARD!

 "LET'S GET HIM UP HERE, BOYS, PLAY HIS THEME!" "OH, I'M PUTTING ON MY HOMBURG, PUTTING ON MY REP TIE, PUTTING ON MY–" YAY! **HERE HE COMES!** PHWEET! "WELL GOSH-GEE, GOSH–"

 "AND AS A BONUS SURPRISE – SIT-TING OUT FRONT UNBEKNOWNST TO BERNARD IS HIS FORMER DANCING PARTNER, **MISS GINGER MURCH!** GINGER! GINGER! PHWEET! "GINGER!" "BERNARD!"

 "I WAS A FOOL GINGER!" "WE WERE BOTH FOOLS, DARLING! BUT WHAT DOES IT MATTER? WE'RE **TOGETHER AGAIN!**"

 "TOGETHER AGAIN! TELL THE WORLD THAT WE'RE TOGETHER AGAIN! THROUGH THE STORMY WEATHER AGAIN, FOREVER AGAIN, TOGETHER AGAIN!" RAY! PHWEET! RAY!

 "THAT CONCLUDES TONIGHT'S 'LATE, LATE FANTASY.' TUNE IN TOMORROW WHEN YOU WILL BE HUMPHREY BOGART."

 GREAT IDEA FOR A SHOW.

FIRST THING I DO EVERY DAY IS GET UP AND PUT ON MY BODY.

NEXT I SCREW ON MY HEAD, CLIP IN MY EYES, PASTE ON MY NOSE AND CUT OUT A HOLE FOR MY MOUTH.

THEN I SPRAY THE WHOLE THING WITH FIXATIVE AND GO TO WORK.

BY MID-MORNING MY EYES ARE GONE.

BY NOON I'VE LOST THE USE OF MY MOUTH.

BY LATE AFTERNOON, I CAN HARDLY BREATHE THROUGH MY NOSE.

BY QUITTING TIME THE ONLY THING STILL WORKING IS MY BODY.

I DRAG IT HOME AND GIVE IT A BATH. IT WAKES UP.

I GIVE MY HEAD A DRINK. IT WAKES UP.

MY DATE COMES. I SPRAY ON SOME FIXATIVE AND WE GO OUT DANCING.

HE CALLS ME HIS DREAM GIRL.

WILL YOU MARRY ME?   WHY DO YOU ASK ME TO MARRY YOU?

BECAUSE YOU'VE GOT A ROSE IN YOUR TEETH. I'M A FOOL FOR A WOMAN WHO CARRIES A ROSE IN HER TEETH.

BUT WHAT IF I HURT YOU?

OH, WOULD YOU? NOT TOO MUCH OF COURSE. BUT TO BE HURT JUST A LITTLE BY A WOMAN WITH A ROSE IN HER TEETH— WOW!

WHAT IF I WERE UNFAITHFUL?

HOT DIGGETY! TO HAVE A WO-MAN WITH A ROSE IN HER TEETH UN-FAITHFUL TO ME! I-I SOMEHOW NEVER THOUGHT I'D RISE THAT FAR.

WHAT IF I CONSUMED YOU WITH MY STRANGE AND INSATIABLE APPETITES?

OH, BOY! NOT ALL AT ONCE, MIND YOU. BUT A LITTLE BIT AT A TIME BY A WOMAN WITH A ROSE IN HER TEETH—THAT'S MORE THAN I EVER HOPED FOR.

WHAT IF I TOOK THE ROSE OUT OF MY TEETH?

GLADYS!

I'LL PUT IT BACK, GEORGE—LOOK, GEORGE! I PUT IT BACK!

SO HOW DOES IT FEEL?

OH, FINE. FINE. FINE.

YOU LIKE IT?

OH, SURE. I MEAN YOU CAN'T TELL AN AWFUL LOT IN THE BEGINNING.

BUT YOU THINK FROM ALL INDICATIONS IT WAS THE RIGHT MOVE?

WELL, SHE WAS THE NICEST GIRL I'D MET FOR AWHILE.

AND SHE'S HAPPY? SHE SEEMS TO BE HAPPY?

WELL, NEITHER ONE OF US IS A BIG TALKER.

YOU DON'T ASK EACH OTHER IF YOU'RE HAPPY?

WELL, NEITHER ONE OF US IS VERY DEMONSTRATIVE.

BUT YOU LOVE EACH OTHER?

LOVE? I DON'T KNOW. WHEN YOU'RE AN ADULT YOU MAKE CONCESSIONS.

BUT IT IS BETTER THAN BEING SINGLE?

WELL, I WILL SAY THIS. YOU'RE LESS LONELY.

LUCKY DOG! IF I COULD MEET A GIRL LIKE THAT I'D GET MARRIED TOO.

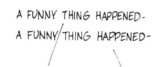

UH.

UM.

A FUNNY THING HAPPENED—
A FUNNY THING HAPPENED—

HA HA— WE BOTH SPOKE AT THE SAME TIME.

HA HA, YOU GO FIRST.

NO. NO. YOU GO FIRST.

NO, YOU GO FIRST.

WELL, LET'S SEE— WELL— I DON'T REMEMBER WHAT I WAS GOING TO SAY.

I WENT SHOPPING TODAY. I BOUGHT BUTTER.

I NEED MORE SOCKS. I'M RUNNING LOW ON SOCKS.

THE PHONE RANG FOUR TIMES THIS MORNING WHILE I WAS VACUUMING. THEY HUNG UP BEFORE I COULD ANSWER.

UM.

UM.

CHECK SIR.

THAT WAS LOVELY GEORGE.

WE REALLY HAVE TO GET AWAY FROM THE KIDS MORE OFTEN.

ONE NIGHT, DRIVING HOME TO EVENING COCKTAILS, I WAS — SUDDENLY STRUCK THROUGH THE WINDSHIELD BY THE RAYS OF THE FULL MOON.

AND I GREW BODY HAIR, POINTED EARS, — CLOVEN HOOVES, AND A TAIL.

AND I THOUGHT "AT **LAST!** IT'S THE **REAL** ME!" AND WITH FEAR SECRETLY MINGLED WITH DELIGHT I ARRIVED HOME —

WHERE MY WIFE SAID "YOUR DINNER'S COLD — AND STOP LOOKING AT ME IN THAT ACCUSING WAY!"

AND MY SON SAID, "ALL THE OTHER DADDIES ARE GOOD AT FIXING THINGS, YOU'VE GOT FINGERS LIKE **CLAWS!**"

AND MY LITTLE GIRL SAID, "WHY DO I HAVE TO HAVE THE ONLY FATHER ON THE BLOCK WHO'S **DIFFERENT**?"

SO I ATE THEM ALL UP.

WEREWOLVES REALLY SHOULDN'T MARRY.

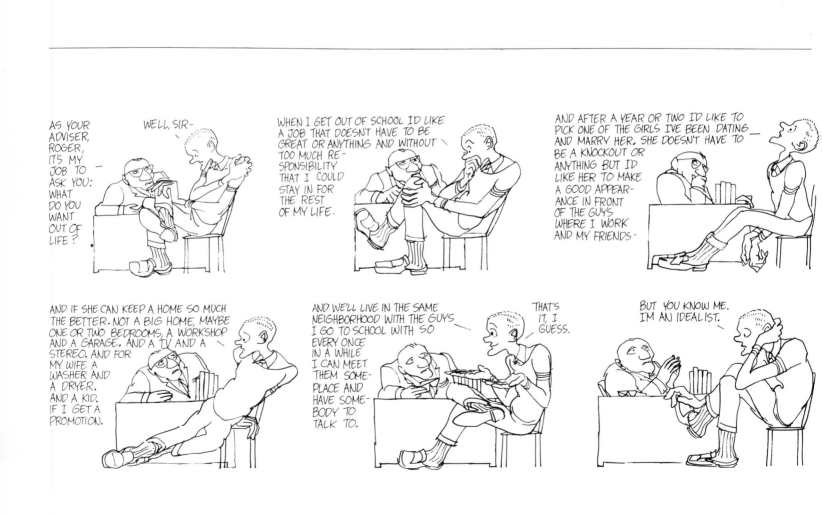

AS YOUR ADVISER, ROGER, IT'S MY JOB TO ASK YOU: WHAT DO YOU WANT OUT OF LIFE?

WELL, SIR—

WHEN I GET OUT OF SCHOOL I'D LIKE A JOB THAT DOESN'T HAVE TO BE GREAT OR ANYTHING AND WITHOUT TOO MUCH RESPONSIBILITY THAT I COULD STAY IN FOR THE REST OF MY LIFE.

AND AFTER A YEAR OR TWO I'D LIKE TO PICK ONE OF THE GIRLS I'VE BEEN DATING AND MARRY HER. SHE DOESN'T HAVE TO BE A KNOCKOUT OR ANYTHING BUT I'D LIKE HER TO MAKE A GOOD APPEARANCE IN FRONT OF THE GUYS WHERE I WORK AND MY FRIENDS—

AND IF SHE CAN KEEP A HOME SO MUCH THE BETTER. NOT A BIG HOME, MAYBE ONE OR TWO BEDROOMS, A WORKSHOP AND A GARAGE. AND A TV AND A STEREO. AND FOR MY WIFE A WASHER AND A DRYER. AND A KID. IF I GET A PROMOTION.

AND WE'LL LIVE IN THE SAME NEIGHBORHOOD WITH THE GUYS I GO TO SCHOOL WITH SO EVERY ONCE IN A WHILE I CAN MEET THEM SOMEPLACE AND HAVE SOMEBODY TO TALK TO.

THAT'S IT, I GUESS.

BUT YOU KNOW ME. I'M AN IDEALIST.

A DANCE TO SUMMER.  IN THIS DANCE I SYMBOL- IZE THE RESTLESS- NESS OF NEW - SEASONS.

 THE DESIRE TO ESCAPE- FROM BOREDOM-  FROM RESPONSI- BILITY-  FROM COOL MEN-  FROM ALL THE IN- ADEQUATE PLEASURES

THE DESIRE TO LIFT ONESELF OUT OF THE PREDICT- ABLE -  AND NEVER HAVE TO RETURN.

  SOME DANCER.

JERRY DOWN AT THE OFFICE, HE'S FOOLING AROUND BE- HIND HIS WIFE'S BACK WITH RENEE THE BOOK- KEEPER. YOU KNOW WHAT I TELL HIM?  JOHN, I'M GOING CRAZY.

I SAY TO HIM: "JERRY I DON'T UNDERSTAND YOU GUYS WHO GO FOOLING AROUND WITH OTHER - WOMEN. MY JOANNIE IS SIX DIFFERENT KINDS OF WOMEN AND THAT'S ENOUGH FOR ONE MAN.  PLEASE LISTEN, JOHN.

"SHE'S A WIFE, MOTHER, SISTER, DAUGHTER, SWEETHEART, - BEST FRIEND.' HOW MANY WOMEN CAN A GUY WANT?  JOHN, I'M GOING CRAZY.

"EVERY NIGHT," I TELL HIM, "IT'S A NEW EXPERIENCE. FOR FIFTEEN YEARS I COME HOME, JOANNIE'S WAITING THERE WITH A SURPRISE."  PLEASE LISTEN FOR ONCE, JOHN.

SO HERE I AM HOME, BABY. WHO YOU GONNA BE FOR JOHN TONIGHT?  MYSELF.

WHY, WHEN I'M IN SUCH A GOOD MOOD, - DO YOU HAVE TO START A FIGHT?

I DON'T KNOW WHAT YOU'RE TRYING TO PULL BUT AS LONG AS I'VE GONE **THIS** FAR YOU MAY AS WELL KNOW THE **COMPLETE** TRUTH- TO **ME** YOU'RE A **ONE NIGHT** ADVENTURE!

AND **THAT'S** WHAT YOU ARE TO **ME**, HONEY! AFTER ALL **I'M** MARRIED **TOO**.

YOU- MARRIED?

SURE-

I- I DIDN'T KNOW-

WANT TO SEE MY KIDS?

NO-**NO**! FOR GODSAKES- PLEASE **DON'T**!

LOOK, SUGAR- YOU WANT TO FORGET THE WHOLE THING?

YOU WON'T THINK I'M **UNMANLY**?

HONEY, TO ME YOU'RE A **TIGER**.

WHAT A TRULY WONDERFUL PERSON

IF I WEREN'T HAPPILY MARRIED THAT LITTLE GIRL'S HUSBAND WOULD HAVE TO LOOK OUT.

A DANCE TO — 1966.

THIS YEAR'S DANCE — ATTEMPTS A MORE **SOPHISTI-CATED** APPROACH THAN MY DANCES OF PREVIOUS YEARS.

IT REJECTS THE TOO EASY — ALIENATION OF MY DANCE OF '65.

IT ELIMINATES THE STYLISH DISILLUSION — OF MY DANCE OF '64.

IT SHUNS THE BOAST-FUL NON-CONFORMITY OF MY — DANCE OF '63.

IT DENIES THE — EGOISTIC IDEALISM OF MY DANCES OF '62, '61, '60 AND '59.

THIS YEAR'S DANCE — IS STRICTLY PRAGMATIC.

REALISTIC IN — ITS APPRAISAL OF THE WORLD UNSENTIMENTAL IN ITS SUMMING UP OF MY POSITION IN IT.

A DANCE TO 1966

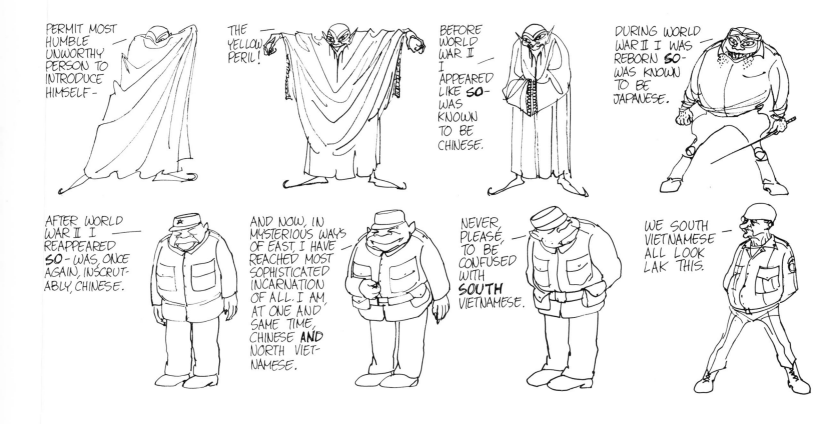

PERMIT MOST HUMBLE UNWORTHY PERSON TO INTRODUCE HIMSELF —

THE — YELLOW PERIL!

BEFORE WORLD WAR II I — APPEARED LIKE **SO** — WAS KNOWN TO BE CHINESE.

DURING WORLD WAR II I WAS — REBORN **SO** — WAS KNOWN TO BE JAPANESE.

AFTER WORLD WAR II I — REAPPEARED **SO** — WAS, ONCE AGAIN, INSCRUT-ABLY, CHINESE.

AND NOW, IN MYSTERIOUS WAYS OF EAST, I HAVE — REACHED MOST SOPHISTICATED INCARNATION OF ALL. I AM, AT ONE AND SAME TIME, CHINESE **AND** NORTH VIET-NAMESE.

NEVER, PLEASE, — TO BE CONFUSED WITH **SOUTH** VIETNAMESE.

WE SOUTH VIETNAMESE — ALL LOOK LAK THIS.

SIR, WE'VE RECEIVED ANOTHER SIGNAL FROM HANOI.

HANOI HINTS IT MAY BE WILLING TO COME TO THE CONFERENCE TABLE ONCE IT HAS STRONGER ASSURANCES OF YOUR CREDIBILITY.

HANOI HINTS IT MIGHT TRUST YOUR CREDIBILITY WERE YOU TO CONCEDE THAT EACH TIME THERE'S BEEN A BOMBING PAUSE U.S. CASUALTIES HAVE ACTUALLY **DROPPED.**

WHERE DO THEY GET THEIR FIG-URES?

FROM THE DEPARTMENT OF DEFENSE.

TAKE A SIGNAL.

TO HANOI?

TO THE DEPARTMENT OF DEFENSE.

FIX THE FIGURES.

IN FEBRUARY OF 1965, IN ORDER TO GET HANOI TO THE NEGOTIATING TABLE, WITH HEAVY HEART I ORDERED MY BOMBERS TO STRIKE NORTH VIETNAM.

THIS STRATEGY PROVED IN MANY WAYS SUCCESS-FUL. BUT IT DID NOT GET HANOI TO THE NEGO-TIATING TABLE.

IN JULY OF 1966, IN ORDER TO GET HANOI TO THE NEGOTIATING TABLE, WITH SOMBRE DISMAY I ORDERED MY BOMBERS TO STRIKE HANOI AND HAIPHONG.

THIS STRATEGY PROVED IN MANY WAYS EFFECTIVE. BUT IT DID NOT GET HANOI TO THE NEGOTIATING TABLE.

IN JANUARY OF 1967, IN ORDER TO GET HANOI TO THE NEGOTIATING TABLE, WITH MANIFEST SOBRIETY I ORDERED MY BOMBERS TO TAKE OUT CHINA'S NUCLEAR CAPABILITY.

THIS STRATEGY PROVED IN MANY WAYS FRUITFUL. BUT IT DID NOT GET HANOI TO THE NEGOTIATING TABLE.

IN JULY OF 1967, IN ORDER TO GET HANOI TO THE NEGOTIATING TABLE, WITH THE AGONY OF POWER I ORDERED MY BOMBERS TO STRIKE PEKING.

NOW, AT THIS VERY MOMENT, MY MISSILES ARE RELUC-TANTLY ALERTED FOR MOSCOW.

LET ME WARN HANOI—

MY RESTRAINT IS NOT INEXHAUSTIBLE.

IN WORLD WAR I A GUY WANTED TO DISSENT — WE RIOTED ON HIM, PUT HIM ON TRIAL, THREW HIM IN JAIL.

IN WORLD WAR II A GUY WANTED TO DISSENT — WE BEAT HIM UP, LOST HIM HIS JOB, SCORNED HIM IN FRONT OF HIS FAMILY AND NEIGHBORS.

IN KOREA A GUY WANTED TO DISSENT — WE BRANDED HIM A COMMIE, DESTROYED HIS CAREER, MADE HIM CRAWL BEFORE CONGRESS.

BUT IN VIETNAM A GUY WANTS TO DISSENT — WE LET HIM TEACH IN OUR SCHOOLS, HAVE A PARADE, PUBLISH IN OUR NEWSPAPERS.

WHEN DO WE GET RID OF — ALL THIS CODDLING —

AND RETURN TO OUR HALLOWED — TRADITIONS?

WE WORKED A LIFETIME AND WHAT HAVE WE GOTTEN OUT OF IT?   I AM POLARIZING THE SOCIETY.

GAVE YOU EVERYTHING YOU EVER WANTED. NEVER ASKED FOR ANYTHING IN RETURN.   I AM COMMITTING ACTS OF CIVIL DISOBEDIENCE IN ORDER TO DISRUPT THE POWER STRUC- TURE.

WENT DEEP INTO DEBT TO SEND — YOU TO COLLEGE.   UNTIL I AM BRUTALLY SUPPRESSED THEREBY EXPOSING THE VIOLENCE THAT LIES BENEATH THE MASK OF CORPORATE LIBERALISM.

SO YOU GO ON STRIKE, TAKE OVER THE UNI- VERSITY AND GET SENT TO JAIL.   THUS RADICALIZING THE MIDDLE CLASS BY REVEALING THE OPPRESSIVE NATURE OF THE SYSTEM.

AND BREAK YOUR PARENTS' HEART.   FORCING THE MIDDLE CLASS TO CHOOSE BETWEEN REVOLUTION AND ENSLAVEMENT.

YOU MUST BE VERY HAPPY.   WOULD I BE DOING THIS IF IT WASN'T GOOD FOR YOU?

IN THE EARLY THIRTIES JUST ABOUT ALL THE FRIENDS I WENT TO COLLEGE WITH WERE IDEALISTS.

IN THE EARLY FORTIES HALF THE IDEALISTS I WENT TO COLLEGE WITH WERE EXPOSED BY THE **OTHER** HALF AS UNDERGROUND TROTSKYITES.

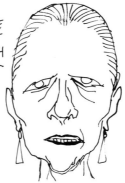

IN THE EARLY FIFTIES ALL THE UNDERGROUND TROTSKYITES I WENT TO COLLEGE WITH EXPOSED THE REST OF THE IDEALISTS I WENT TO COLLEGE WITH AS UNDERGROUND COMMUNISTS.

IN THE EARLY SIXTIES HALF THE COMMUNISTS I WENT TO COLLEGE WITH WERE EXPOSED BY THE OTHER COMMUNISTS I WENT TO COLLEGE WITH AS INFORMERS FOR THE F.B.I.

IN THE MID-SIXTIES HALF THE TROTSKYITES I WENT TO COLLEGE WITH TURNED OUT TO BE AGENTS FOR THE C.I.A.

THANK HEAVEN FOR DRUGS ON CAMPUS. —

WE COULDN'T SURVIVE ANOTHER GENERATION OF IDEALISTS.

POLITICS IS A LIE.

SO I DROPPED OUT OF POLITICS.

POLITICS USES HISTORY.

SO I QUIT STUDYING HISTORY.

HISTORY IS PRINTED IN BOOKS.

SO I QUIT READING BOOKS.

BOOKS ARE MADE UP OF WORDS.

SO I QUIT KNOWING WORDS.

Give to the Pure

Panel 1. LOOK OUT IN THE STREET, CHARLIE - SOME LADY'S BEING CHASED BY A GUY WITH A ROCK.

PROBABLY LOVERS. DON'T GET INVOLVED, DORIS.

Panel 2. HE CAUGHT HER. BOY, WILL YOU LISTEN TO HER SCREAM.

MIND YOUR OWN BUSINESS AND SHUT THE WINDOW, DORIS.

Panel 3. I WONDER IF WE SHOULD CALL THE POLICE.

DON'T BOR-ROW TROUBLE. THE FIRST THING THEY WANT IS YOUR NAME.

Panel 4. YEAH. THEN THEY PRINT IT IN THE PAPERS AND YOU START GET-TING WEIRDO PHONE CALLS.

YEAH. ABSO-LUTELY NO CONSID-ERATION.

Panel 5. YEAH. ANY-HOW IT'S OVER. SHE'S JUST LYING THERE.

COME AWAY FROM THE WINDOW, DORIS. IT'S NOT OUR BUSINESS.

Panel 6. HEY, LOOK ACROSS THE STREET, CHARLIE - SOME GUYS CLIMBING OUT ON THE WINDOW LEDGE.

Panel 7. WHERE?

THERE.

Panel 8. JUMP! JUMP! JUMP! JUMP! JUMP!

Panel 9. IT'S TIME, AMERICA, FOR "**WHAT DO YOU WANT TO BE WHEN YOU GROW UP?**" THE FUN SHOW THAT ANSWERS THAT **BOTHERSOME** QUESTION-"WHERE DID I GO WRONG?" WHO'S OUR FIRST GUEST, FRANK?

HI, STEPPING BEFORE OUR NATION WIDE SELF HELP CAMERAS IS MRS. E.S.P. OF PATCHOGUE, L.I.

Panel 10. AND WHAT IS IT YOU WANTED TO BE WHEN **YOU** GREW UP, MRS. E.S.P.?

I COULD NEVER MAKE UP MY MIND. I USED TO WANT TO BE AN OPERA SINGER.

Panel 11. AN OPERA SINGER OF SONGS! HOW DOES **THAT** RATE ON THE AMBITION METER, AUDIENCE?

RAH

BUT I COULDN'T SEEM TO GET STARTED. THEN I WANTED TO BE A NOVELIST.

Panel 12. A NOVELIST OF BOOKS! HOW DOES THAT SCORE, AUDIENCE?

RAH

BUT I COULDN'T SEEM TO GET STARTED. IN THE MEANTIME I HAD GROWN UP TO BE THE ONE THING I NEVER WANTED TO BE- A MOTHER.

Panel 13. A MOTHER OF CHILDREN! SCORE THAT ONE, AUDIENCE!

RAH RAH RAH RAH RAH

BUT THAT'S WHERE I WENT **WRONG!** IT'S HARD WORK. IT'S TOO MUCH RESPONS-IBILITY!

Panel 14. HA! HA! WE'RE ALL SURE YOU'RE A **WON-DER-FUL** PARENT, MRS. E.S.P.

IT GIVES ME NO TIME FOR MYSELF. I DON'T KNOW WHO I **AM** ANYMORE!

Panel 15. WON-DER-FUL! BUT IN YOUR HEART OF HEARTS ISN'T A **MOTHER** WHAT **ALL** YOU DEAR LADIES WANT TO BE? 'FESS UP, MRS. E.S.P. NOW 'FESS UP!

BUT NOW I **KNOW** WHAT I WANT TO BE! A **TAP** DANCER IN THE MOVIES WITH FRED ASTAIRE! NOT DANCING IN THE MOVIES WITH FRED ASTAIRE IS WHERE I WENT WRONG. YOU SAID YOU'D HELP ME. YOU SAID—

Panel 16. HA! HA! AMERICA KNOWS YOU'RE PULLING ITS LEG, MRS. E.S.P. AND AS A BONUS FOR COMING ON OUR SHOW WE'RE GIV-ING YOU ANOTHER CHILD! ISN'T THAT **WON-DER-FUL**, AUDIENCE?

RAHHHHHHHH

THIS WAY, LADY.

"MAKE NICE, BABY. MAKE NICE," THEY SAY.

THEN THEY TAKE MY HAND AND PAT THEM- SELVES ON THE CHEEKS.

"DOES BABY LOVE MOMMY? DOES BABY LOVE DADDY?" THEY SAY.

THEN THEY PRESS ME AGAINST THEIR FACES TILL I CAN'T EVEN BREATHE.

"MOMMY LOVES BABY. DADDY LOVES BABY," THEY SAY.

THEN **SHE** GRABS A PIECE OF FACE AND **HE** GRABS A PIECE OF ARM AND THE BOTH OF THEM SQUEEZE.

"MOMMY AND DADDY **DON'T** LOVE BABY WHEN BABY IS NAUGHTY," THEY SAY.

THEN I GET SENT OUT WITH THE MAID.

WHATEVER THAT WORD "LOVE" MEANS —

I CAN HARDLY WAIT TILL I'M BIG ENOUGH TO DO IT TO **THEM.**

SHE KEEPS — PUSHING ME TO GET AHEAD.

SO HE TELLS ME I DON'T MAKE A NICE HOME FOR HIM.

SO SHE ACCUSES ME OF — BEING WEAK.

SO HE TELLS ME I'VE — LOST MY LOOKS.

SO SHE TELLS ME IF SHE WERE A MAN SHE'D BE — MAKING TWICE AS MUCH AS I DO!

SO HE ACCUSES ME OF BEING A TERRIBLE — MOTHER!

SO SHE SAYS IT WASN'T — HER IDEA TO HAVE A KID!

SO I GET SENT TO MY ROOM FOR BEING BAD.

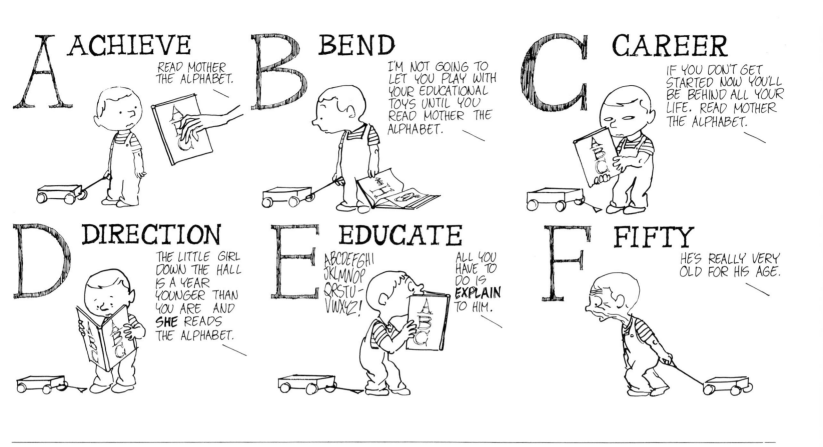

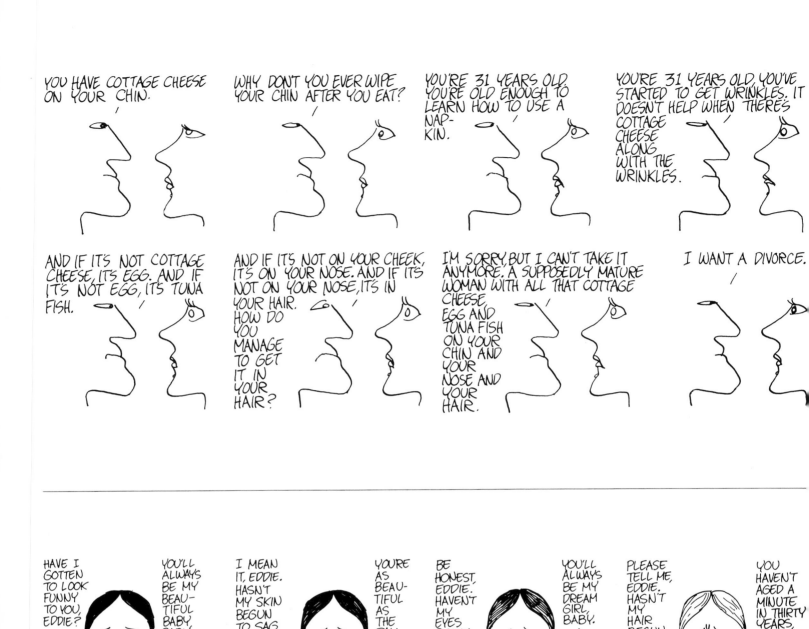

YOU HAVE COTTAGE CHEESE ON YOUR CHIN.

WHY DON'T YOU EVER WIPE YOUR CHIN AFTER YOU EAT?

YOU'RE 31 YEARS OLD. YOU'RE OLD ENOUGH TO LEARN HOW TO USE A NAP-KIN.

YOU'RE 31 YEARS OLD. YOU'VE STARTED TO GET WRINKLES. IT DOESN'T HELP WHEN THERE'S COTTAGE CHEESE ALONG WITH THE WRINKLES.

AND IF IT'S NOT COTTAGE CHEESE, IT'S EGG. AND IF IT'S NOT EGG, IT'S TUNA FISH.

AND IF IT'S NOT ON YOUR CHEEK, IT'S ON YOUR NOSE. AND IF IT'S NOT ON YOUR NOSE, IT'S IN YOUR HAIR. HOW DO YOU MANAGE TO GET IT IN YOUR HAIR?

I'M SORRY, BUT I CAN'T TAKE IT ANYMORE. A SUPPOSEDLY MATURE WOMAN WITH ALL THAT COTTAGE CHEESE, EGG AND TUNA FISH ON YOUR CHIN AND YOUR NOSE AND YOUR HAIR.

I WANT A DIVORCE.

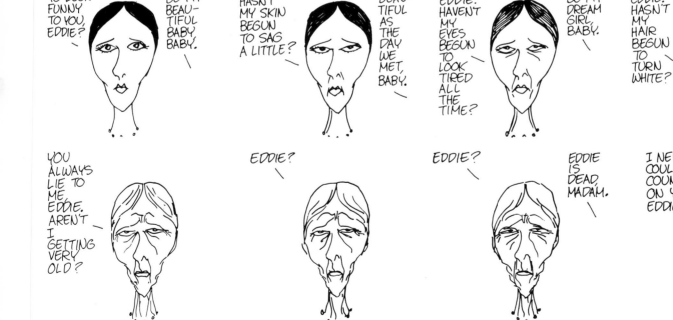

HAVE I GOTTEN TO LOOK FUNNY TO YOU, EDDIE?

YOU'LL ALWAYS BE MY BEAU-TIFUL BABY BABY.

I MEAN IT, EDDIE. HASN'T MY SKIN BEGUN TO SAG A LITTLE?

YOU'RE AS BEAU-TIFUL AS THE DAY WE MET, BABY.

BE HONEST, EDDIE. HAVEN'T MY EYES BEGUN TO LOOK TIRED ALL THE TIME?

YOU'LL ALWAYS BE MY DREAM GIRL, BABY.

PLEASE TELL ME, EDDIE. HASN'T MY HAIR BEGUN TO TURN WHITE?

YOU HAVEN'T AGED A MINUTE IN THIRTY YEARS, BABY.

YOU ALWAYS LIE TO ME EDDIE. AREN'T I GETTING VERY OLD?

EDDIE?

EDDIE?

EDDIE IS DEAD, MADAM.

I NEVER COULD COUNT ON YOU, EDDIE.

I USED TO THINK I WAS POOR.

THEN THEY TOLD ME I WASN'T POOR, I WAS **NEEDY**.

THEN THEY TOLD ME IT WAS SELF-DEFEATING TO THINK OF MYSELF AS NEEDY, I WAS **DEPRIVED**.

THEN THEY TOLD ME DEPRIVED WAS A BAD IMAGE, I WAS **UNDERPRIVILEGED**.

THEN THEY TOLD ME UNDERPRIVILEGED WAS OVERUSED. I WAS **DISADVANTAGED**.

I STILL DON'T HAVE A DIME.

BUT I HAVE A **GREAT** VOCABULARY.

WHY MUST IT GO ON, BEN? ALL THIS FIGHTIN', ALL THIS VIOLENCE?

SOMEDAY THERE'LL BE A TOWN HERE, TESSIE—

AN' THERE'LL BE A CHURCH, AN' THERE'LL BE A SCHOOL, AN' THERE'LL BE LAW—

AN' THERE'LL BE HORSELESS CARRIAGES, AN' THERE'LL BE FACTORIES, AN' THERE'LL BE AIR POLLUTION—

AN' THERE'LL BE ALIENATION, AN' THERE'LL BE DROP-OUTS, AN' THERE'LL BE VIOLENCE. **THAT'S** WHAT WE'RE FIGHTIN' FOR, TESSIE—

A HERITAGE.

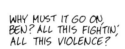

A DANCE
TO 1967. —

IN THIS
DANCE
I HAVE —
SYMBOL-
IZED A
NATION
IN FLUX—

ESTABLISH-
ING FRESH
APPROACHES
TO THE
PROBLEMS
OF —

POVERTY—

CRIME IN
—THE STREETS—

VIETNAM— —

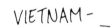

AND CIVIL
RIGHTS. —

A DANCE TO 1967.

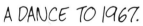

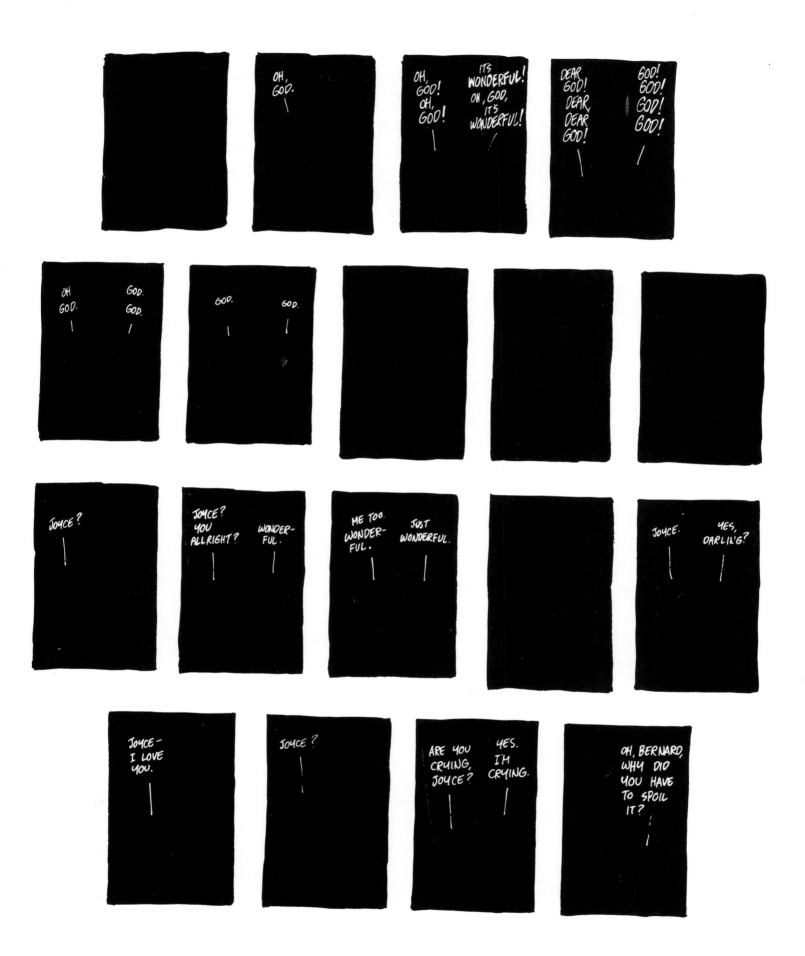

YOU'RE THROUGH WHITEY! **FINISHED!** **DEAD!** A REVOLUTION IS SWEEPING THE WORLD AND YOU'RE **OUT** OF IT!

NOTHING YOU CAN DO TO SAVE YOURSELF, WHITEY! **DON'T** OFFER ME YOUR WHITE MARCHING! YOUR WHITE PICKETING! YOU'RE NOT GETTING OFF THE HOOK OF HISTORY **THAT** EASY, BABY!

YOU'RE DYING OF ROT, WHITEY! YOUR MEN ARE AUTOMATONS, YOUR WOMEN, DEATH MASKS! YOU SAY YOU WANT TO HELP **ME**? YOU CAN'T EVEN HELP **YOURSELF**, WHITEY!

DON'T YOU SEE HOW I HATE YOU, WHITEY? **YOU** LIBERAL REFORMERS! **YOU** CRIPPLED POWER STRUCTURE! I SCORN YOU, WHITEY! I REVILE YOU!

THAT WILL BE $1.50 APIECE, GENTLEMEN.

SAME TIME, NEXT WEEK?

OH, PLEASE!

AS A MATTER OF RACIAL PRIDE WE WANT TO BE CALLED "BLACKS." —

WHICH HAS REPLACED THE TERM "AFRO-AMERICAN" —

WHICH REPLACED "NEGROES"— —

WHICH REPLACED "COLORED PEOPLE" —

WHICH REPLACED "DARKIES"— —

WHICH REPLACED "BLACKS." —

AND NOW THE LATEST NEWS FROM OVERSEAS.

FIGHTING CONTINUES TONIGHT IN NEW YORK'S HARLEM. THE GOVERNMENT OF THE UNITED STATES HAS FILED A STRONG PROTEST WITH THE GOVERNMENT OF GHANA CLAIMING THAT IT ACTED ILLEGALLY IN DISPATCHING TWO THOUSAND MARINES TO PROTECT THE HOTEL THERESA AND OTHER STRATEGIC POINTS IN THE COMMUNITY.

IN THE MEANTIME THE GOVERNMENT OF ISRAEL HAS ANNOUNCED PLANS TO DROP ONE THOUSAND PARATROOPS INTO THE BOROUGHS OF BROOKLYN AND BRONX TO PROTECT HOUSES OF WORSHIP.

IN FURTHER DEVELOPMENTS FRENCH PARATROOPS HAVE REFUSED TO WITHDRAW THEIR OCCUPATION OF FIFTY FRENCH RESTAURANTS ON THE ISLAND OF MANHATTAN UNTIL ALL PERSONNEL ARE EVACUATED.

PRESIDENT JOHNSON CONTINUES TO INSIST THAT NEW YORK IS AN INTERNAL PROBLEM AND THAT IF FOREIGN TROOPS DON'T WITHDRAW IMMEDIATELY, AMERICAN TROOPS WILL FORCE THEM OUT —

JUST AS SOON AS THEY GET BACK FROM VIETNAM, THAILAND, JAPAN, TAIWAN, LAOS, THE CONGO, GUANTANAMO, GUATEMALA, AND SANTO DOMINGO.

FIRST THE **NEGROES** REVOLTED.

THEN THE **PUERTO RICANS** REVOLTED.

THEN THE **YOUTH** REVOLTED.

THEN THE **INTELLECTUALS** REVOLTED.

IN ORDER TO PRESERVE **LAW** AND **ORDER** I HAVE HAD TO PUT THEM ALL IN JAIL.

BUT PUNITIVE MEASURES ARE **NOT ENOUGH.** THESE TROUBLED TIMES **CRY OUT** FOR **NEW** ANSWERS TO UNSOLVED **OLD** PROBLEMS.

TO SEEK OUT THE **CAUSES** OF ANARCHY AND PROPOSE A **CURE** I HAVE — THIS DAY APPOINTED A **FACT FINDING COMISSION.**

TO THIS COMISSION I AM APPOINTING 1 **DEMOCRAT,** 1 **REPUBLICAN,** 1 **YOUNG PERSON,** 1 **OLD PERSON,** 1 **INTELLECTUAL,** 1 **ANTI-INTELLECTUAL,** 1 **NEGRO** AND 1 **BIGOT.**

COME LET US REASON TOGETHER.

IN MY OPINION NEGROES ARE GOING TOO FAR WITH THEIR PROTESTS.

MAY I QUOTE YOU, MR. BACKLASH?

NO. THIS IS OFF THE — RECORD.

THEN, SIR, **ON THE RECORD** YOU ARE **FOR** INTEGRATION?

ON THE RECORD I'M EVEN FOR **DEMOCRACY**, SONNY.

THEN **OFF** THE RECORD YOU'RE **AGAINST** DEMOCRACY, MR. BACKLASH?

OFF THE RECORD I'M ONLY FOR **ME**, SONNY. TOO MANY YEARS SPENT WORRYING ABOUT **OTHER** PEOPLE.

CAN YOU SPECIFY MR. BACKLASH?

TOO MANY YEARS BEING A **LIBERAL** — TRYING TO FIX UP THE REST OF THE WORLD. IS THE REST OF THE WORLD GRATEFUL? SURE, TELL ME ANOTHER ONE, SONNY!

YOU FEEL UNAPPRECIATED, MR. BACKLASH?

THEY ALL **HATE** US, SONNY! FOREIGNERS HATE US. STRANGERS HATE US. NEGROES HATE US. AND WE HATE THEM. IT'S EVEN-STEVEN, SONNY. DROP THE BOMB, SAY I!

ON **WHO** EXACTLY, MR. BACKLASH?

ON EVERYBODY BUT ME, SONNY. A NEW BROOM SWEEPS CLEAN.

MAY I QUOTE ANY OF THIS, MR. BACKLASH?

FOR THE RECORD, SONNY, YOU MAY SAY THAT IN **MY** OPINION EXTREMIST TACTICS ARE LOSING THE NEGROES THEIR MANY MODERATE FRIENDS.

THANK YOU, MR. WHITEY BACKLASH.

I DUG JAZZ —

AND WHITEY PICKED UP ON IT.

I DUG HIP —

AND WHITEY PICKED UP ON IT.

I DUG ROCK —

AND WHITEY PICKED UP ON IT.

I DUG FREEDOM —

AND FINALLY LOST WHITEY.

ONE NATION—

UNDER GOD—

INDIVISIBLE

BIG DADDY—THAT LOOK ON YER FACE—YER **HIDIN'** SOME-THIN'—

SIT DOWN, CHILD. YEW GONN'A HAVE T'BE BRAVE.

IT'S **GREAT SOCIETY!** SOMETHIN'S HAPPENED T'**GREAT SOCIETY!**

GREAT SOCIETY HAS HAD AN ACCIDENT, CHILD.

BUT IT COULD ON'Y BE A LI'L BITTY ACCIDENT WITH YEW LOOKIN' AFTER GREAT SOCIETY THE WAY YEW ALWEEZ SWORE Y'WOULD, BIG DADDY.

GREAT SOCIETY HAS GONE AWAY, HAS GONE T'SLEEP, HAS GONE TO A BETTER LAND'N YEW AN' I KNOW OF, CHILD.

HOW C'D THERE BE A BETTER LAND'N THIS HERE LAND, BIG DADDY? I WANT T'GO WITH GREAT SOCIETY!

GREAT SOCIETY WOULDN'T WANT **THAT**, CHILD. GREAT SOCIETY'D WANT US T'CARRY ON WITHOUT HIM EVEN EF IT MEANS GIVIN' UP SOME O' HIS DREAMS.

BUT I ALWEEZ THO'T YEW **LOVED** GREAT SOCIETY'S DREAMS, BIG DADDY!

BIG DADDY LOVES WHAT HE C'N AFFORD T'LOVE, CHILD. THAT'S WHAT WE CALL GROW-IN' UP.

THIS ACCIDENT O' GREAT SOCIETY'S, BIG DADDY— HAS IT **ALREADY** HAPPENED— OR ARE **YEW** ABOUT T'HAVE IT HAP-PEN?

NAOW, WE DON'T WANT T'GROW UP **TOO** FAST, CHILD.

ONE DAY A LITTLE BOY WENT TO
SEE THE EMPEROR ON PARADE
AND SAW RIDING, GRINNING,
AND WAVING IN A BUBBLE
DOMED CARRIAGE A GIANT
OF A MAN WHO WAS STARK
NAKED.

"WHY" EXCLAIMED THE
LITTLE BOY, " THE EMPEROR
HAS **NO** CLOTHES!"

TO WHICH A WISE MAN REPLIED, "WHILE
IT IS **JUST** CRITICISM TO QUARREL
WITH THE EMPEROR IN HIS **TASTE** IN
CLOTHES, IT IS **IRRESPONSIBLE**
CRITICISM TO SAY HE IS NAKED
BECAUSE THAT APPROACH FAILS TO
OFFER AN ALTERNATIVE."

"BESIDES," SAID A SECOND WISE
MAN, "HOW CAN YOU BE SO SURE
THAT THE EMPEROR DOESN'T HAVE
ACCESS TO MATERIAL THAT WE
DON'T HAVE? WHAT YOU'RE
REALLY OBJECTING TO IS **STYLE**."

TO THIS A THIRD WISE MAN ADDED,
"WHETHER OR NOT THE EMPEROR
SHOULD HAVE GONE INTO THE
STREET WITHOUT CLOTHES IS NOW
MERELY A DEBATER'S POINT. THE
FACT IS THAT HE IS THERE, AND
WE ARE COMMITTED."

WHERE UPON ALL THE WISE MEN
CALLED FOR UNITY IN THE FACE
OF DIVISIVENESS WHILE REMIND-
ING THEMSELVES OF THE IMPORT-
ANCE OF TOLERATING THE LITTLE
BOYS DISSENT.

OR, AS THE EMPEROR WHO
HAD TAPED THE DIALOGUE
WAS TO LATER PUT IT,
"ONLY IN AN ATMOSPHERE
OF FREE DEBATE CAN WE
DETERMINE THE FACTS."

MORAL: THE EMPEROR
HAS CLOTHES, YOU
BETTER BELIEVE IT.

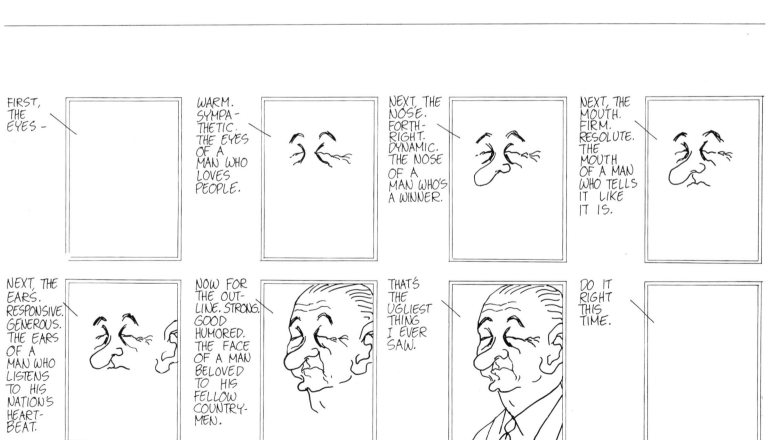

MY VIEW ON VIETNAM IS THAT THE U.S. ESCALATIONS OF '65-'67 ARE IN CLEAR VIOLATION OF THE GENEVA ACCORDS OF '54, THE EISENHOWER LETTER OF '56 AND THE KENNEDY POLICY RE-EVALUATION OF LATE '63.

AND THEREFORE WE SHOULD — END OUR INTERVENTION.

MY VIEW ON THE ARAB-ISRAELI WAR IS THAT U.S. INACTION WAS IN CLEAR VIOLATION OF THE U.N. MANDATE OF '48 DEFILES — THE DULLES PLEDGE OF '56 AND DENIES THE JOHNSON-WILSON COMMITMENT OF '67.

THEREFORE WE SHOULD HAVE — INTERVENED.

FOREIGN POLICY IS MAINLY A — MATTER OF DISCOVERING ONE'S OWN EMOTIONAL BIAS —

AND THEN — CITING HISTORY.

From "Baby and Child Care" by Doctor Benjamin Spock: "DO YOU WORRY WHEN YOUR TWO YEAR OLD PULLS ANOTHER'S HAIR, OR PLAYS WITH A TOY PISTOL?"

"IF YOUR CHILD IS HURTING ANOTHER OR LOOKS AS IF HE WERE PLANNING MURDER, PULL HIM AWAY... AND GET HIM INTERESTED IN SOMETHING ELSE."

"IT'S BETTER NOT TO HEAP SHAME ON HIM — THAT ONLY MAKES HIM FEEL ABANDONED AND MORE AGGRESSIVE."

"IF A CHILD GOES ON BEING UNUSUALLY AGGRESSIVE... AND DOESN'T SEEM TO BE LEARNING ANYTHING ABOUT COOPERATIVE PLAY..."

"IF HE'S SPENDING A GOOD PART OF EACH DAY TELLING ABOUT IMAGINARY ADVENTURES, NOT AS A GAME BUT AS IF HE BELIEVES IN THEM..."

"IT RAISES THE QUESTION WHETHER HIS REAL LIFE IS SATISFYING ENOUGH."

OH, WE OFFER SOME WONDERFULLY SAFE CHOICES ON VIETNAM. THOSE OF OUR CLIENTS WHO'VE ABANDONED CIVIL RIGHTS TELL US A STAND ON VIETNAM IS **JUST** WHAT THEY NEED TO FEEL RIGHTEOUS AGAIN.

I'D HATE TO WASTE MY OUTRAGE ON ANOTHER LOSER.

WHAT **WE** RECOMMEND IS A STAND JUST A **SMIDGIN** TO THE LEFT OF THE PRESIDENT'S. YOU APPROVE OF HIS **MOTIVES** BUT NOT HIS **METHODS.**

SAY, THAT'S THE STAND I TOOK ON **McCARTHY!** IT WAS A **WINNER!**

IT LOOKS **SMASHING** ON YOU!

A LITTLE **LESS BOMBING**

MM-I'VE ALREADY FORGOTTEN ABOUT NEGROES.

Dear Mr. President:
I am resigning from your administration for reasons of conscience.

I can no longer be a party to policies which I feel are tearing the country apart.

Many who have **served you loyally** over the **years** are increasingly bitter and despondent **over** the direction you are taking.

When these men resigned the reasons invariably given were "family problems" and "ill health".

This public **evasiveness** is, to my mind, as immoral as the policies which they condemn.

Therefore, despite fear of personal and political retribution, I will make my objections to your dangerous policies public the moment I resign.

Dear Mr. President:
Serious family problems and the state of my own health force me with great reluctance to submit

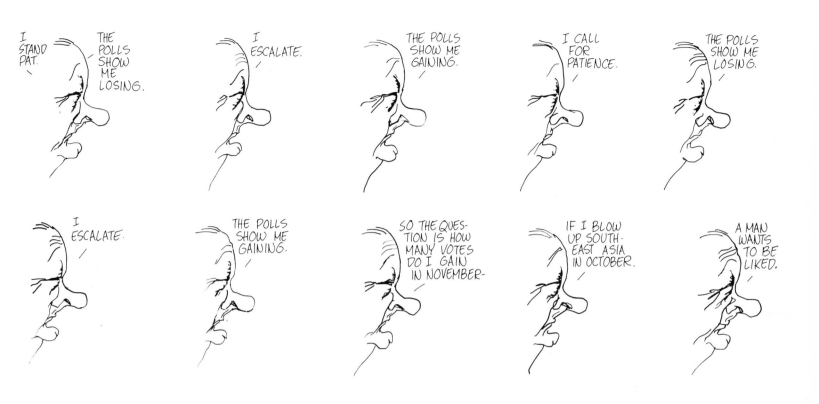

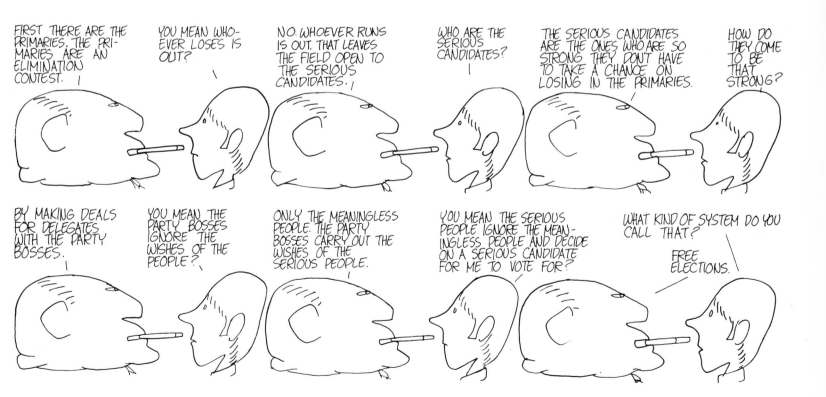

AN ESCALATING WAR.

RISING POVERTY.

RISING RACISM.

RIOTS IN THE GHETTOS.

CRIME IN THE STREETS.

DRUGS ON THE CAMPUS.

A SPREADING DIS-ILLUSIONMENT WITH ELECTORAL POLITICS.

IN NOVEMBER, IN ORDER TO SOLVE THESE PROBLEMS-

I CAN VOTE FOR RICHARD NIXON OR LYNDON JOHNSON.

IN A FREE SOCIETY THERE IS ALWAYS A CHOICE.

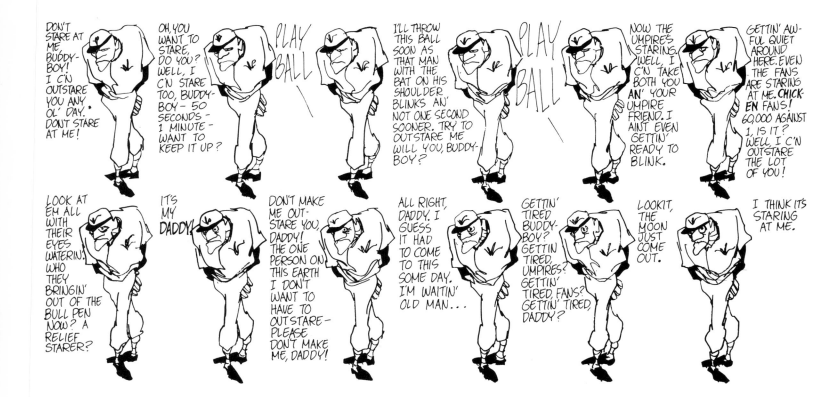

THESE ARE THE BOBBY TWINS. ONE IS A GOOD BOBBY. ONE IS A BAD BOBBY.

THE GOOD BOBBY IS A COURAGEOUS REFORMER. THE BAD BOBBY MAKES DEALS.

1.

2.

THE GOOD BOBBY SENT FEDERAL TROOPS DOWN SOUTH TO ENFORCE CIVIL RIGHTS. THE BAD BOBBY APPOINTED RACIST JUDGES DOWN SOUTH TO ENFORCE CIVIL RIGHTS.

THE GOOD BOBBY IS A FERVENT CIVIL LIBERTARIAN. THE BAD BOBBY IS A FERVENT WIRE TAPPER.

3.

4.

THE GOOD BOBBY IS ILL AT EASE WITH LIBERALS. THE BAD BOBBY IS ILL AT EASE WITH GROWNUPS.

IF YOU WANT ONE BOBBY TO BE YOUR PRESIDENT YOU WILL HAVE TO TAKE BOTH... FOR BOBBIES ARE WIDELY NOTED FOR THEIR FAMILY UNITY.

5.

6.

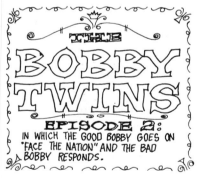

MAKE YOUR MOVE, RINGO! BANG!

CLICK

EAT LEAD, YOU LOUSY STOOLIE! BANG!

CLICK

DIE YOU CRUDDY JAP! RATATATAT!

CLICK

BANG BANG BANG BANG BANG BANG BANG GET A DOCTOR! SENATOR KENNEDY'S BEEN SHOT!

CLICK

MY SONIC GUN WILL FINISH YOU OFF, SPACE MAN! ZAP!

CLICK

'NIGHT, HONEY.

SWEET DREAMS, DEAR.

THE FIRST MAN WENT INTO THE VOTING BOOTH AND YELLED AT THE MACHINE FOR THREE MINUTES..

THE SECOND MAN WENT INTO THE VOTING BOOTH AND FELL ASLEEP FOR THREE MINUTES..

THE THIRD MAN WENT INTO THE VOTING BOOTH AND BECAME ILL FOR THREE MINUTES..

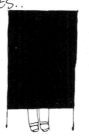

THE FOURTH MAN WENT INTO THE VOTING BOOTH AND SCRATCHED OUT ALL THE PRESIDENTIAL CANDIDATES NAMES IN THREE MINUTES..

THE FIFTH MAN WENT INTO THE VOTING BOOTH AND KICKED THE MACHINE TO PIECES.

"I ACCEPT THE MANDATE OF THE PEOPLE," SAID THE PRESIDENT-ELECT..

AND BUOYED BY THE CHEER OF HIS SUPPORTER MADE PLANS TO UNIFY THE COUNTRY.

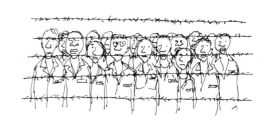

VIETNIXON

I, and many like me, cleaved our political identities out of the war in Vietnam. We felt a certain post–Joe McCarthy giddiness in knowing that the only strong opposition to Johnson's war in those early years was Dr. Spock, I. F. Stone, Robert Lowell, *The New York Review of Books*, a handful of Harvard and Berkeley students and a tiny peace movement made up of several thousand smiling, thoroughly middle-class peace marchers.

We were the left, and Johnson and Rusk and Bundy and McNamara were the enemy—and we teached-in and marched and took full-page ads and refused invitations to the White House and accepted invitations to just about every other party and felt very much in the vanguard. And then we woke up in the late '60s to find ourselves outflanked on our own left. We discovered that, according to the kids, we were nothing more than liberal, no more radical than James Reston, no more of a threat to those in power than Arthur Schlesinger, Jr.

By 1968, my extremist facade was in tatters. I found myself talking tradition, responsibility and pragmatism to would-be building burners and bomb throwers. At the age of 40 I listened defensively to 22-year-old Weatherwomen explaining Marxism-Leninism. I listened to 20-year-old counterculture journalists lecturing me on revolution and rock lyrics. Quietly, I built up a thirst for Glenn Miller records. I took both sides on such issues as student occupation of buildings: You could occupy but you couldn't make a mess. I deplored the violation of First Amendment rights of Washington VIPs who were shouted down on campuses—but couldn't wait to see it happen again. I deplored the bombing of ROTC buildings but couldn't wait to see it happen again. I was passionate, but didn't identify; I felt less than a man for sticking to booze and shunning dope.

Nixon was my salvation. He brought the revolution to its knees and released me into a world that I once more understood. I won't say that I was grateful, but I didn't have it in me to hate him, certainly not the way I hated LBJ. Johnson had betrayed me, but everyone knew what to expect from Nixon. He had been with us an eternity. No surprises, no disappointments. He was a turd, a wonderful turd—for a cartoonist, the King of Turds. From his Checkers speech to his "You won't have Nixon to kick around anymore" speech to his farewell to the White House staff speech, he was a genius of the second-rate, the Mozart of mediocrity.

Nixon masterminded our further dissolution. Always an adversarial politician, he found new and devious ways to divide us, deceive us, lie to us. He honed Johnson's worst weaknesses until he made them his own: He bombed, he invaded, he spied on us. He was wonderful to draw. His unintegrated parts invited endless comment: uneasy head atop wind-up toy body. Nothing on Nixon fit right: tab A went into slot B. And well he knew it. There are no shirtsleeve photos, even his strolls on the beach were in full dress. I am sure that, naked, he wore knee socks; in the shower, boxer shorts.

Watergate improved him. His eyes darted like pinballs. His battered head drooped low on his tin body. His shoulders met his eyebrows, his arms waved like tollgates, his legs like prosthetic devices. He was our favorite sick joke. But the joke was on us.

He gave us what he called his "Vietnamization Program," only the wrong country got Vietnamized. America got Vietnamized. Before Vietnamization, most Americans believed in our leaders; after Vietnamization, we believed in the corruption of our leaders. Before Vietnamization, we believed in our future; after Vietnamization, we even quit believing in our past. Before Vietnamization, we saw ourselves as idealists and winners; after Vietnamization, we saw ourselves as pragmatists and survivors. The dream of racial equality was replaced by the threat of racial equality, the dream of abundance by fantasies of scarcity. Before Vietnamization, kids wanted to grow up to be president; after Vietnamization, kids gave up on the idea, fearful of indictment. Before Vietnamization, we had in this country a concept of nationhood. It was replaced by concepts of neighborhood. America could barely call itself a country anymore. Hostile tribes, feudal fiefdoms, covert operations, search-and-destroy missions, enclaves for the privileged, strategic hamlets for the poor.

What the media described as "the tragedy of Watergate" gave many of us great pleasure. Nixon's fall, an old-fashioned morality tale, had us cheering and screaming. "More!" we cried. "More tapes! More evasions!" Before a mob of children at Disney World he announced, "I am not a crook." What was a 12-year-old to make of that? One more nail in the coffin of the American Dream. One more by-product of Vietnamization.

Nixon's rise and fall and rise and fall and rise and fall is the great soap opera of American public life. He has been a focus of national attention longer than any politician in our history. But, always the loser, he was overshadowed even in his own time. Since the 1950s, the political agenda of the United States has been largely set by our reactions to communist states. In terms of lasting effect, the most influential politician on the scene in the Nixon years was Ho Chi Minh.

Once upon a time there were the 1960s during which:

HE GOT SHOT.

HE GOT SHOT.

HE GOT SHOT.

HE GOT SHOT.

HE GOT SHOT.

HE GOT SHOT.

HE GOT ELECTED.

AND HE GOT ELECTED.

"THE DISEASE OF OUR TIME IS AN ARTIFICIAL AND MASOCHISTIC SOPHISTICATION — THE VAGUE UNEASINESS THAT OUR VALUES ARE FALSE."
Spiro T. Agnew

DICK 'N' PAT

DICK, BETTER GET A MOVE ON! COMPANY'S COMING FOR DINNER!

BE THERE IN TWO SHAKES OF A LAMB'S TAIL, PAT. WHO'S COMING?

THE CHAIRMAN OF THE BOARD OF GENERAL DYNAMICS, THE PRESIDENT OF CHASE MANHATTAN, THE CHAIRMAN OF THE BOARD OF LOCKHEED—

GEE, PAT.

THE CHAIRMAN OF THE BOARD OF GENERAL MOTORS, THE CHAIRMAN OF THE BOARD OF U.S. STEEL, THE PRESIDENT OF I.B.M., A COLORED MAN —

VERY GOOD, PAT.

AND DAVID AND JULIE.

DAVID'S COMING! WELL, I'LL BE DARNED, PAT!

DICK, WHEN WE HAVE COMPANY I WISH YOU'D STOP CALLING DAVID "SIR".

BUT, PAT, HE'S THE PRESIDENT'S GRANDSON!

DICK, YOU'RE THE PRESIDENT.

I KNOW, PAT, BUT I MEAN THE **REAL** PRESIDENT.

DICK, I WISH YOU'D GET IT INTO YOUR HEAD THAT THIS ISN'T A MOVIE.

I WISH YOU WOULDN'T TALK THAT WAY, PAT.

IF **THIS** ISN'T A MOVIE THIS COUNTRY'S IN A LOT MORE TROUBLE THAN YOU THINK.

A DANCE TO AUTUMN.

IN THIS DANCE I CELEBRATE—

I CELEBRATE—

UM — I CELEBRATE—

CELEBRATE—

I CELEBRATE **SURVIVAL!**—

A DANCE TO AUTUMN.

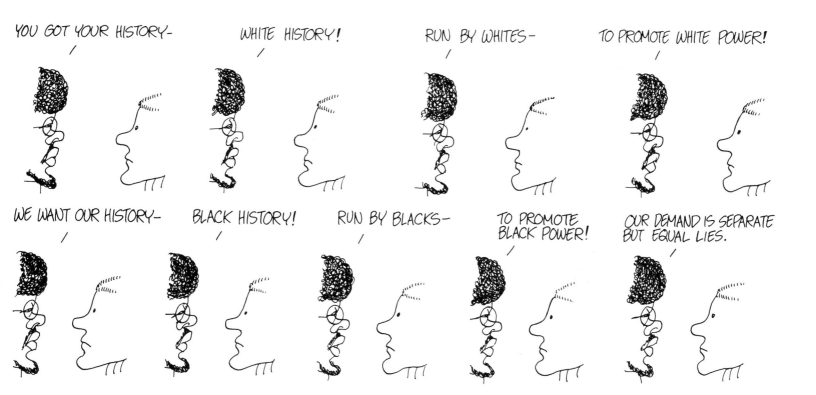

LAWS ARE DESIGNED TO PROTECT SOCIETY.

WHEN CRIMINALS BREAK THE LAW AND GET AWAY WITH IT—

THE RESULT IS RISING VIOLENCE, CRIME IN THE STREETS, ANARCHY.

WHEN BIG CORPORATIONS BREAK THE LAW AND **DON'T** GET AWAY WITH IT—

THE RESULT IS FALLING STOCKS, RISING UNEMPLOYMENT, CRIME IN THE STREETS, ANARCHY.

SO PROSECUTE CRIMINALS!

AND SUPPORT CORPORATE CRIME!

KEEP AMERICA STRONG!

A DANCE TO AUTUMN.

IN THIS DANCE I CELEBRATE A RETURN TO EDUCATION.

A RETURN TO REASON.

A RETURN TO DIALOGUE.

A RETURN TO ORDER.

A DANCE TO AUTUMN.

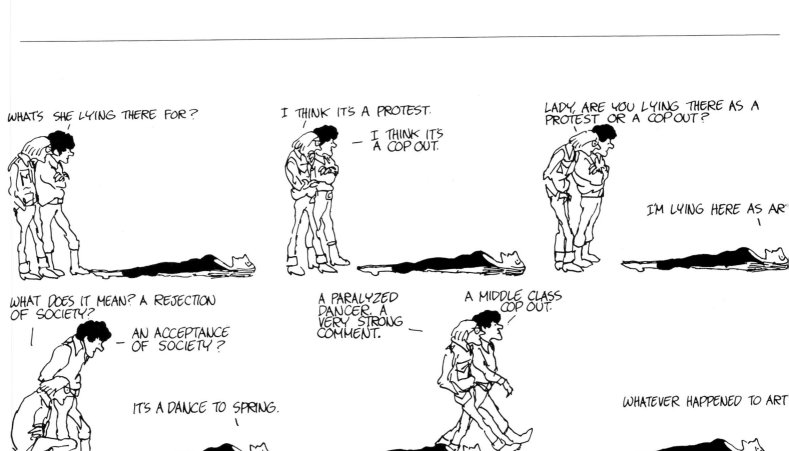

DO YOU TAKE THIS WOMAN TO OPPRESS, SUBJUGATE, BRUTALIZE —

AND REDUCE TO A CONDITION OF SERVITUDE AND SECOND CLASS CITIZENSHIP?

I DO.

DO YOU TAKE THIS MAN TO ALIENATE, DOMINATE, EMASCULATE —

AND REDUCE TO A STATE OF ABJECT GUILT AND CHILD LIKE DEPENDENCE?

I DO.

I NOW PRONOUNCE YOU HUSBAND AND WIFE.

NOW   WE WORK IT OUT.

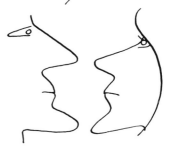

YOU WANTED TO GET MARRIED. I DIDN'T.

WE GOT MARRIED.

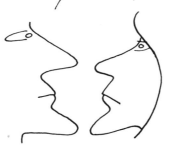

YOU WANTED KIDS. I DIDN'T.

WE HAD KIDS.

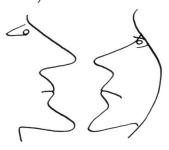

NOW YOU TELL ME I'M YOUR OPPRESSOR AND YOU WANT TO BE LIBERATED.

O.K., YOU'RE LIBERATED.

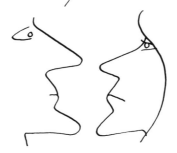

CAN I GO NOW?

BY
MYSELF —

I FEEL
LONELY.

WITH OTHER
PEOPLE —

I FEEL
ISOLATED.

THE ANSWER
MAY BE —

TO JOIN MY
LONELINESS
TO   MY
ISOLATION.

A DANCE TO SUMMER.   INFLATION —   DEPRESSION —   REPRESSION —   REVOLUTION —

POLLUTION —   SEGREGATION —   AMERICA!   HEADS OFF! THERE
                                                    GOES THE FLAG.

ESCALATION —

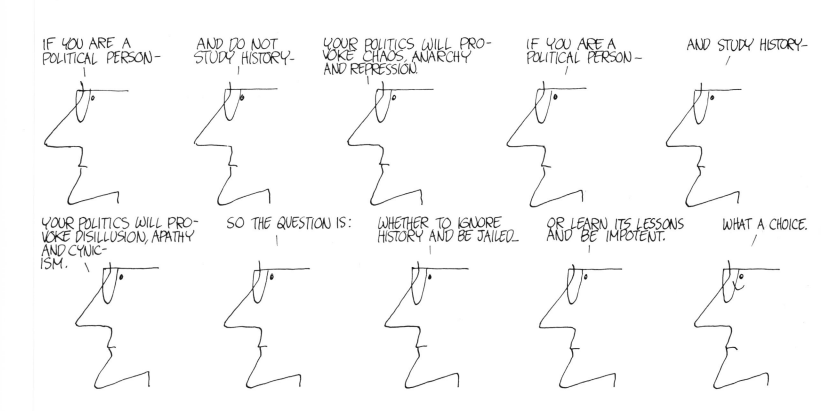

EVERY CHRISTMAS THE FAMILY GATHERS TOGETHER—

AND FIGHTS ABOUT PRESENTS—

MONEY—

AND WHY WE DON'T SEE EACH OTHER MORE OFTEN.

AND IT OCCURS TO ME THAT THE BIBLE MUST HAVE ITS DATES WRONG.

CHRIST WAS BORN ON GOOD FRIDAY.

AND CRUCIFIED ON CHRISTMAS.

ISN'T EVERYBODY?

THE DAY I MET IRENE I WAS SURE I HAD MET MY DREAM GIRL.

"DON'T THINK OF ME AS YOUR DREAM GIRL," IRENE WARNED ME. "IF YOU DO I'M BOUND TO DISAPPOINT YOU."

BUT I TOLD IRENE, "THAT'S EXACTLY WHAT MY DREAM GIRL WOULD SAY." AND WE GOT MARRIED.

AFTER SEVEN YEARS I SAID TO IRENE, "ALL WE EVER TALK ABOUT IS MONEY AND I'VE COME TO THE CONCLUSION YOU'RE NOT MY DREAM GIRL."

SO I LEFT IRENE TO THINK THINGS OVER. WHAT I DECIDED WAS THAT WHILE IRENE HAD HER SHORTCOMINGS SHE STILL HAD A BETTER BODY THAN ALL MY FRIENDS' WIVES.

WHEN I RETURNED HOME THIS DUMPY MIDDLE-AGED WOMAN ANSWERED THE DOOR. "WHERE'S IRENE?" I DEMANDED.

"I'M IRENE," SHE SAID. SO I THREW HER OUT!

I DON'T CARE HOW LONG SHE KNOCKS, I'M NOT LETTING IN ANY STRANGERS UNTIL THE IRENE I SETTLED FOR COMES HOME.

I THOUGHT SCHOOL WAS A JAIL.

UNTIL I GOT A JOB. BOY, WAS THAT A JAIL!

THEN I GOT MARRIED. EVEN MORE OF A JAIL!

UNTIL I GOT DRAFTED INTO THE ARMY. THE WORST JAIL YET!

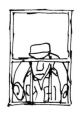

UNTIL I GOT IN TROUBLE AND WENT TO JAIL—

AND LEARNED THAT JAIL IS EVEN MORE OF A JAIL THAN SCHOOL, A JOB, MARRIAGE, OR THE ARMY.

SO FINALLY I KNOW WHAT FREEDOM'S ALL ABOUT:

THE RIGHT TO CHOOSE WHICH JAIL.

WHEN I WAS A KID—

I USED TO DREAM OF WHAT I WANTED TO BE AS A GROWNUP.

A TEST PILOT—

A COWBOY—

A BALL PLAYER.

NOW I'M FORTY.

AND I'M NOT A TEST PILOT—

I'M NOT A COWBOY—

I'M NOT A BALL PLAYER—

AND I'M NOT A GROWNUP.

WHO EVER DREAMED IT WOULD BE THIS HARD?

IT WAS WRONG FOR US TO GET INTO VIETNAM—

BUT WE'D LOSE FACE IF WE GOT OUT.

I'M FOR SAVING AMERICAN LIVES—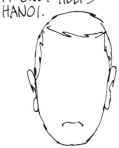

BUT TALKING ABOUT IT ONLY HELPS HANOI.

I'M IN SYMPATHY WITH THE ARGUMENTS OF THE PRO-TESTERS.

BUT DEMONSTRATING AGAINST THE GOVERN-MENT IS UN-PATRIOTIC.

I SUPPORT THE PRESIDENT.

BUT I WISH HE'D CHANGE HIS POL-ICIES.

I AM THE VOICE OF MODERATION.

STOP ME BEFORE I KILL MORE.

AMERICANS WILL REMAIN IN INDO CHINA AS LONG AS THERE ARE P.O.W.S.

AMERICANS WILL FIGHT IN INDO CHINA AS LONG AS THERE ARE P.O.W.S.

AMERICANS WILL BE TAKEN PRISONER IN INDO CHINA AS LONG AS THERE ARE P.O.W.S.

ALL P.O.W.S WILL REMAIN IN INDO CHINA AS LONG AS THERE ARE P.O.W.S.

ALL AMERICAN PRESIDENTS WILL REMAIN IN INDO CHINA AS LONG AS THERE ARE P.O.W.S.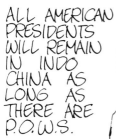

WE ARE ALL P.O.W.S.

THE AMERICAN PEOPLE ARE TIRED OF VIETNAM.

SO WE WON'T TALK ABOUT IT ANYMORE.

THE AMERICAN PEOPLE ARE UNINFORMED ABOUT LAOS.

SO WE WON'T TALK ABOUT IT ANYMORE.

THE AMERICAN PEOPLE ARE FED UP WITH CIVIL RIGHTS.

SO WE WON'T TALK ABOUT THEM ANYMORE.

WHAT WILL WE TALK ABOUT?

POLLUTION.

VIETNAM IS DEAD AS AN ISSUE. THE REAL ISSUE IS ECOLOGY.

BUT WHAT CAN WE DO ABOUT IT?

WE HAVE TO CONTROL THE ENVIRONMENT.

BUT HOW CAN WE DO THAT?

WE HAVE TO CONTROL POLLUTION.

BUT HOW CAN WE DO THAT?

WE HAVE TO CONTROL INDUSTRIAL WASTE.

BUT HOW CAN WE DO THAT?

WE HAVE TO CONTROL INDUSTRY.

OH, YOU MEAN SOCIALISM.

ECOLOGY IS DEAD AS AN ISSUE.

Dear Mom,

Please stop worry-ing about me.

My morale is high,

I am off drugs,

I am out of combat,

I am out of Vietnam,

I am in Sweden.

Your loving son,

THE WAY **THEY** TREAT P.O.W.s IS —  BARBARIC!

THE WAY **WE** TREAT P.O.W.s IS — 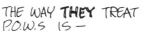 HUMANE!

THEIR TERRORISM SHOWS —  A CALLOUS DISREGARD FOR HUMAN LIFE!

OUR BOMBING RAIDS SHOW —  A DESIRE TO SHORTEN THE WAR AND BRING THE TROOPS HOME!

THE WAY **THEY** NEGOTIATE IS —  DECEITFUL, UNFRUITFUL, AND OFFERS NOTHING NEW!

THE WAY **WE** NEGOTIATE IS —  IN GOOD FAITH!

NOW, THIS IS WHAT I CALL A REALLY SUCCESSFUL PRESS CONFERENCE.  THANK YOU, MR. PRESIDENT!

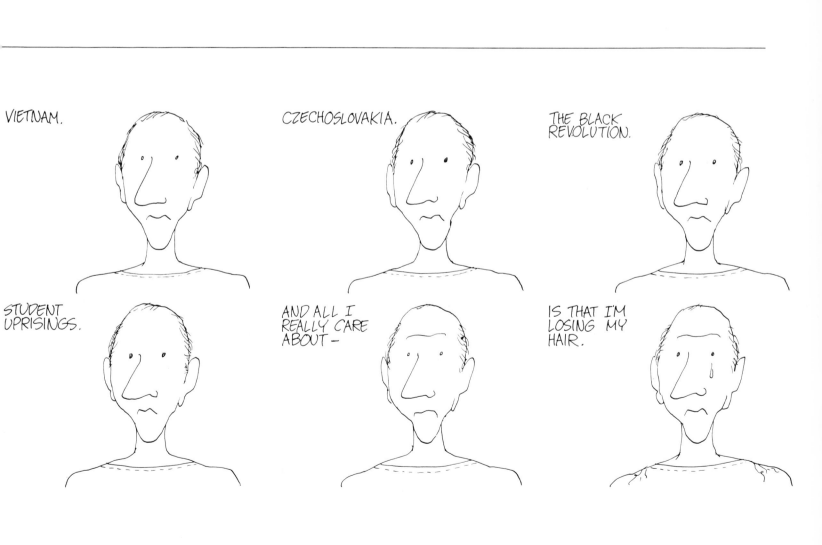

A DANCE TO SUMMER.

IN THIS DANCE I CELEBRATE BECOMING! BECOMING A FREER ME!

A MEDITATING ME.

A LOSING WEIGHT ME.

A MORE IN TOUCH WITH MY BODY ME.

AN EATING PROPER FOODS ME.

AN **ENTIRELY** NEW ME ME!

INSTEAD OF THE OLD ME, DEAD ME, REJECTED ME, DISGUSTING ME— FAT ME, COMPULSIVE ME...

UGLY ME, DEPRESSED ME, SELF-HATING ME

ROTTEN SICK PUTRESCENT

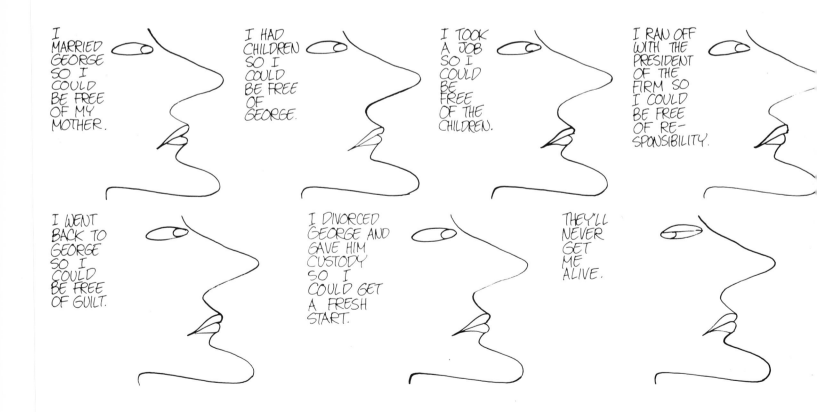

I MARRIED GEORGE SO I COULD BE FREE OF MY MOTHER.

I HAD CHILDREN SO I COULD BE FREE OF GEORGE.

I TOOK A JOB SO I COULD BE FREE OF THE CHILDREN.

I RAN OFF WITH THE PRESIDENT OF THE FIRM SO I COULD BE FREE OF RESPONSIBILITY.

I WENT BACK TO GEORGE SO I COULD BE FREE OF GUILT.

I DIVORCED GEORGE AND GAVE HIM CUSTODY SO I COULD GET A FRESH START.

THEY'LL NEVER GET ME ALIVE.

A DANCE TO AUTUMN.

IN THIS DANCE I CELEBRATE THE NEW ME.

FREE TO BREAK OUT OF OLD MOLDS.

FREE TO EXPERIMENT IN UN-TRADITIONAL WAYS.

FREE TO ESCAPE THE PRISONS OF MY PAST—

THE CHAINS OF MY WOMANHOOD.

FREE TO STRETCH THE LIMITS OF MY IMAGI-NATION.

IT'S NOT WORTH IT.

I COME TO A DOOR. I FEEL JUMPY.

I GO THROUGH. I FEEL BRAVE.

I COME TO ANOTHER DOOR. I FEEL FRIGHT-ENED.

I GO THROUGH. I FEEL STRONG.

I COME TO ANOTHER DOOR. I FEEL LOST.

I GO THROUGH. I FEEL MA-TURE.

I COME TO AN-OTHER DOOR. I FEEL HYSTERI-CAL.

I GO THROUGH. I FEEL IN CON-TROL.

I COME TO ANOTHER DOOR. I FEEL CRAZY.

I REFUSE TO GO THROUGH.

THESE DOORS ARE KILLING ME.

WHEN THEY DRAGGED ME TO SCHOOL AT 5, I REMEMBER SCREAMING: BUT I'M NOT READY

WHEN THEY SENT ME TO CAMP AT 10, I REMEMBER SCREAMING: BUT I'M NOT READY!

WHEN THEY DRAFTED ME AT 19, I REMEMBER SCREAMING: BUT I'M NOT READY!

WHEN THEY MARRIED ME OFF AT 23, I REMEMBER SCREAMING: BUT I'M NOT READY!

WHEN THEY MADE ME A FATHER AT 24, 25, 26 AND 27 I REMEMBER SCREAMING: BUT I'M NOT READY — NOT READY NOT READY NOT READY!

FINALLY, AT 50, I RAN AWAY FROM MY WIFE, MY KIDS AND MY GRANDCHILDREN.

I'M NOT COMING OUT AGAIN TILL I'M READY.

DADDY! — GRANPA! — GEORGE!

ENVY  HAS GIVEN ME A SENSE OF PURPOSE  A MOTIVE TO COMPETE  AND THE DRIVE TO CLIMB TO THE TOP.  IF I DIDN'T HAVE ENVY I WOULDN'T HAVE POWER AND I WOULDN'T BE ENVIED

BY EVERYBODY ELSE WHOSE SENSE OF PURPOSE  MOTIVATES THEM TO COMPETE WITH ME  AND CLIMB TO THE TOP.  TRUST ENVY.  IT MAKES THE SYSTEM WORK.

A DANCE — TO SUMMER.  IN THIS DANCE — I CELEBRATE TORPOR

SITTING AROUND. |

LYING AROUND. /

GETTING A TAN. /

TURNING OVER. |

THANK GOD FOR ART. /

WHAT I LEARNED IN SCHOOL THIS YEAR.

I LEARNED HIGH SCHOOL IS CALLED SECONDARY EDUCATION BECAUSE IT TAKES PLACE IN THE SECOND WORLD.

I LEARNED ONLY TO VOLUNTEER WHEN WHAT I HAVE TO SAY AGREES WITH WHAT THE TEACHER HAS TO SAY.

I LEARNED NOT TO BE CURIOUS ABOUT ANYTHING THAT ISN'T ASSIGNED OR THEY CALL YOU A TROUBLE MAKER.

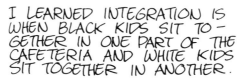

I LEARNED IF YOU HAVE A GOOD TEACHER KEEP IT TO YOURSELF OR THEY GET RID OF HER.

I LEARNED THAT PARENTS HATE TEACHERS ALMOST AS MUCH AS TEACHERS HATE PARENTS BUT NOT AS MUCH AS BOTH HATE KIDS.

I LEARNED INTEGRATION IS WHEN BLACK KIDS SIT TOGETHER IN ONE PART OF THE CAFETERIA AND WHITE KIDS SIT TOGETHER IN ANOTHER.

I LEARNED BUSING IS WRONG —

BECAUSE IT WILL LOWER THE QUALITY OF MY EDUCATION.

SENATOR, WHY DO YOU SUPPORT THE WAR?

SUPPORT THE WAR?! I'M **AGAINST** THE WAR!

I SPEAK IN THE SENATE AGAINST THE WAR!

I SPEAK ON TV AGAINST THE WAR!

I SPEAK TO THE PRESIDENT AGAINST THE WAR!

NOBODY IS MORE OPPOSED TO THE WAR THAN I AM!

THEN WILL YOU VOTE TO CUT MILITARY APPROPRIATIONS?

ARE YOU **CRAZY**? THERE'S A WAR ON!

THE FOLLOWING WORD
TEST IS TO GAUGE YOUR
EMOTIONAL STABILITY.

THE PENTAGON
PAPERS.

MY LAI.

BOMBING DIKES.

DROPPING MORE BOMBS ON
VIETNAM THAN WERE DROPPED
IN WORLD WAR TWO AND KOREA
COMBINED.

HOW
AM I,
DOCTOR?

PERFECTLY
NORMAL.

WHEN I
WAS IN
GRAMMAR
SCHOOL.
VIETNAM.

WHEN I
WAS IN
HIGH
SCHOOL.
VIETNAM.

WHEN I
WAS IN
COLLEGE.
VIETNAM.

WHEN I
GOT
MARRIED.
VIETNAM.

NOW
NO
MORE
VIETNAM.

AND I'M
ONLY
TWENTY-
THREE.

WHAT DO
I DO
WITHOUT
MY
VIETNAM?

COULDN'T FIND A JOB.

JOINED THE ARMY.

SENT TO NAM.

THREE TOURS OF DUTY.

CAME HOME DETESTED.

CAN'T FIND A JOB.

AMNESTY FOR DRAFT DODGERS AND DESERTERS?

THAT'S COOL.

BUT WHAT ABOUT AMNESTY FOR VETS?

I DIDN'T WANT TO BE DRAFTED BUT THREE PRESIDENTS TOLD ME IT WAS MY DUTY.

I DIDN'T WANT TO FIGHT IN VIETNAM BUT THREE PRESIDENTS TOLD ME I WAS DEFENDING FREEDOM.

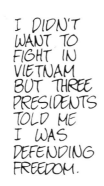

I DIDN'T WANT TO LOSE AN ARM AND A LEG BUT THREE PRESIDENTS TOLD ME IF WE CUT AND RUN WE'D LOSE ALL OF SOUTH EAST ASIA.

THEN THEY SHIPPED ME HOME AND I LEARNED EVERYTHING THREE PRESIDENTS TOLD ME WAS A LIE.

AND NO ONE WILL GIVE ME A JOB BECAUSE I'M A REMINDER AND AN EMBARRASSMENT.

THAT'S WHY I TAKE A HARD LINE ON AMNESTY.

I CAN NEVER FORGIVE THOSE WHO DID NOT HAVE THE GUTS TO DO THEIR DUTY AND SERVE THEIR COUNTRY:

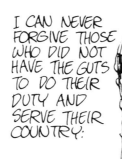 

JOHN KENNEDY, LYNDON JOHNSON AND RICHARD NIXON.

BY THE AGE OF 35 THERE WAS SO LITTLE LEFT OF ME THAT ONE DAY I GOT CAUGHT IN A DRAFT AND FLOATED UP TO THE CEILING.

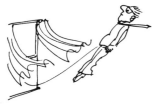

I FLOATED THROUGH THE HOUSE, ENJOYING MY HOME FOR THE FIRST TIME IN YEARS..

UNTIL I CAME TO THE CHILDREN'S ROOM WHERE THE CHILDREN SPOTTED ME AND BEGAN THROWING DARTS.

HOWEVER, THEIR MOTHER SOON PUT A STOP TO THAT. SHE FASTENED A ROPE TO MY WAIST AND TIED ME TO A FENCE IN THE GARDEN.

AT DUSK SHE BROUGHT ME INSIDE AND TIED ME TO A LEG OF THE TV.

AT BEDTIME SHE TIED ME TO THE FOOT OF THE BED AND WENT TO SLEEP, SOBBING.

I DON'T CARE HOW NICE SHE TRIES TO BE...

I'M NEVER COMING DOWN.

I HAD ALWAYS WORN A WINDOW AROUND MY NECK.

IN GOOD SEASONS I OPENED IT.

IN BAD SEASONS I KEPT IT CLOSED.

IN TERRIBLE SEASONS I BOARDED IT UP.

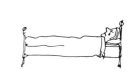

A DOCTOR WARNED ME THAT WITH A WINDOW AROUND MY NECK I MIGHT DIE OF INEXPOSURE.

SO HE TREATED ME FOR IT.

AND AFTER A TIME I WAS CURED.

I NOW WEAR AN ALBATROSS.

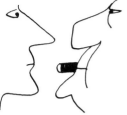

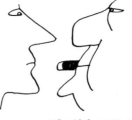

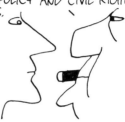

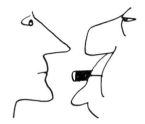
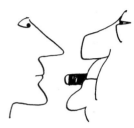

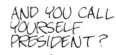

BEHOLD THE KISSINBUNDY.

THE KISSINBUNDY IS AN ADVISOR TO PRESIDENTS IN THE FIELD OF FOREIGN POLICY.

THE FIRST THING A PRESIDENT DOES IN OFFICE...

IS CALL IN THE KISSINBUNDY.

WHO, BASED ON INTELLIGENCE REPORTS AND YEARS OF EXPERTISE...

ADVISES THE PRESIDENT OF HIS OPTIONS.

AFTER EVERYTHING GOES WRONG...

THE PRESIDENT GOES OUT OF OFFICE.

THE FIRST THING THE NEXT PRESIDENT DOES IN OFFICE...

IS CALL IN THE KISSINBUNDY.

THIS NOVEMBER YOU WILL VOTE TO SEE WHICH OF TWO CANDIDATES...

WILL BE ADVISED OF HIS OPTIONS BY THE KISSINBUNDY.

PRESIDENTS CHANGE, BUT KISSINBUNDY..

IS FOREVER.

I WALK ON THE STREET; I FEEL UNSAFE.

I GET ON A BUS; I FEEL UNDESIRABLE.

I GO TO THE OFFICE; I FEEL UNNECESSARY.

I GO HOME; I FEEL UNRECOGNIZED.

I TURN ON TV; I FEEL GOOD ALL OVER.

WATERGATE.

I DO NOT SAY WATERGATE WAS NOT **ILLEGAL**. IT WAS!

BUT I SAY IT IS A BODY BLOW TO THE WHOLE AMERICAN SYSTEM TO SAY IT WAS **CRIMINAL**.

FIRST OF ALL THE PERPETRATORS HELD RESPECTED AND SENSITIVE JOBS IN THE HIGHEST BRANCH OF GOVERNMENT.

NOW I KNOW SOME PEOPLE WOULD CALL THAT CRIMINAL. I DON'T.

NEXT, THEY ARE WHITE, COME FROM GOOD HOMES AND HELD IMPRESSIVE TRACK RECORDS IN PRIVATE ENTERPRISE.

NOW I KNOW SOME PEOPLE WOULD CALL THAT CRIMINAL. I DON'T.

NEXT, THEIR ACTS WERE NOT DIRECTED AT PERSONAL GAIN OR MOB VIOLENCE. NOT AT ALL!

THEIR ACTS, OVER ZEALOUS PERHAPS, WERE DIRECTED AT PERPETUATING FOUR MORE YEARS OF PEACE WITH HONOR AND LAW WITH ORDER.

NOW I KNOW SOME PEOPLE WOULD CALL THAT CRIMINAL. I DON'T.

NO, WATERGATE WAS NOT CRIMINAL. DANIEL ELLSBERG, DR. SPOCK, CHICAGO IN '68 WERE CRIMINAL.

WATERGATE WAS SELF-DEFENSE.

LEFTY, YOU BURGLE ELLSBERG'S SHRINK.

MUGSY, YOU BUG THE WATERGATE.

LOUIE, YOU BURN THE EVIDENCE.

NO-NOSE, YOU SHRED THE MEMOS.

BUTCH, YOU BOMB CAMBODIA.

ANY QUESTIONS?

WHAT IF WE GET CAUGHT?

I DON'T KNOW YA, I NEVER HEARD 'A YA, I DON'T KNOW NUTTIN'.

SCRATCH THE CROWD WHO WANT TO IMPEACH THE PRESIDENT—

AND YOU FIND THE TYPE WHO STOOD AGAINST PEACE WITH HONOR—

AGAINST BRINGING OUR P.O.W.S HOME—

AGAINST NEIGHBORHOOD SCHOOLS—

AGAINST THE RIGHTS OF THE UNBORN.

SO WHEN WE DEFEND THE PRESIDENT IT'S NOT NIXON WE DEFEND—

IT'S OUR VETERANS AND OUR SCHOOLS AND OUR UNBORN AND OUR AMERICAN WAY OF LIFE!

WEAKEN THE OFFICE OF THE PRESIDENCY

AND YOU WEAKEN THE OFFICE OF GOD.

THE MEDIA HAS LEERED AND SNEERED THAT I LOOK TIRED, SWOLLEN-EYED AND OLDER.

THEY SAY IT IS WATERGATE.

BUT IF THE MEDIA HAD BOTHERED TO ASSIGN ONE LONELY REPORTER TO GET THE FACTS STRAIGHT THEY WOULD DISCOVER IT IS NOT WATERGATE.

THEY WOULD DISCOVER THAT EACH YEAR AT THIS TIME I LOOK TIRED, SWOLLEN-EYED AND OLDER.

WHY? ABSURDLY SIMPLE, MY FELLOW AMERICANS. BECAUSE I HAVE **HAY FEVER.**

WATERCHOO

"MANY AMERICANS GOT THE IMPRESSION IN THE SIXTIES THAT THIS WAS AN UGLY COUNTRY RACIST, NOT COMPASSIONATE..

THE ESCALATION IN CRIME AND DRUGS IS A RESULT OF THE MOVEMENT TOWARD PERMISSIVENESS..

THE AVERAGE AMERICAN IS JUST LIKE THE CHILD IN THE FAMILY.

YOU GIVE HIM SOME RESPONSIBILITY AND HE'S GOING TO AMOUNT TO SOMETHING.

YOU PAMPER HIM AND YOU ARE GOING TO MAKE HIM SOFT, SPOILED AND A VERY WEAK CHARACTER...

THIS COUNTRY HAS ENOUGH ON ITS PLATE IN THE WAY OF THROWING DOLLARS AT PROBLEMS...

MORE IMPORTANT THAN MORE MONEY TO SOLVE A PROBLEM IS TO AVOID A TAX INCREASE...

NOW LET US UNDERSTAND. THIS IS NOT A PERFECT COUNTRY."

R.M.N. Nov 9, '72

HE'S CHEWING UP THE CONGRESS!

HE'S DEVOURING THE COURTS!

HE'S SHREDDING THE CONSTITUTION!

WE BETTER GET RID OF HIM!

WE CAN'T!

WHY NOT?

BECAUSE IT WOULD TEAR THE COUNTRY APART!

UP AGAINST THE WALL, PRESIDENT.

LET'S SEE WHAT WE GOT HERE. — $100,000 IN SMALL BILLS AND CHANGE.

A CARTE BLANCHE CARD MADE OUT TO THE NAME OF BEBE REBOZO. A TELEPHONE CREDIT CARD MADE OUT TO THE NAME OF ROBERT ABPLANALP.

A BLUE WORSTED SUIT JACKET WITH THE NAME-TAG: HOWARD HUGHES. UNMADE OUT INCOME TAX FORMS FOR 1970 AND '71.

AND 23 KNIVES, FORKS AND SPOONS FROM THE WHITE HOUSE — DINING ROOM.

11-11

WHAT DO YOU HAVE TO SAY FOR YOURSELF, FELLA? — AGNEW DID IT.

WHAT DO YOU WANT TO BE WHEN YOU GROW UP? — WELL, I DON'T WANT TO BE A PILOT BECAUSE YOU WASTE FUEL.

AND I DON'T WANT TO BE A LAWYER BECAUSE YOU GET INDICTED.

AND I DON'T WANT TO BE A DOCTOR BECAUSE IT'S TOO COMMERCIAL.

AND I DON'T WANT TO BE PRESIDENT BECAUSE IT'S CROOKED.

AND I DON'T WANT TO BE A TEACHER BECAUSE WHO KNOWS WHAT'S TRUE OR FALSE?

SO I DON'T THINK I'LL BE ANYTHING. IT'S THE ONLY MORAL CHOICE.

I STONEWALLED THEM ON THE WAR.

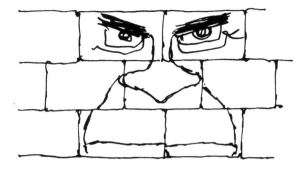

I STONEWALLED THEM ON THE COVER-UP.

I STONEWALLED THEM ON THE TAXES.

I STONEWALLED THEM ON THE TAPES.

I STONEWALLED THEM ON THE COURTS.

I HAVE NOT YET BEGUN TO STONEWALL.

HAPPY HOOLIGAN

"Can you imagine Richard Nixon as president?" people used to say. Everyone laughed. At one time people thought in terms of a recognizable presidential class. This was a thousand years ago, you'll have to take my word for it. Adlai Stevenson was presidential. Dwight Eisenhower was presidential. John F. Kennedy was 15 years too young to be presidential, but, aside from that, maybe. Nelson Rockefeller was presidential. It didn't have to do with politics or talent or brain power. It was a quality hard to define but undoubtedly burned into the national sensibility with FDR.

Richard Nixon is said to have told his advisors he picked Jerry Ford as vice president because Ford was so dumb that he stood as insurance against impeachment. Nixon believed that the country could not imagine Ford president. But by the time we could imagine Nixon president, we could imagine anyone president. Not the first time Nixon screwed himself.

Ford came in riding a wave of hopelessness. No one expected much after Johnson and Nixon. People just wanted peace, in Vietnam and in the streets. They were weary of leadership and liars and CIA machinations and Cold War theology. A mood of disenchantment set in. No one much wanted to talk about it or analyze it. The '60s had been the period for talk, discussions, analysis. Everything that had to be said about the country had been said. Every criticism to be made had been made, over and over. We knew by the middle '70s all about American racism, American imperialism, American atrocities. We knew about our army in Vietnam coming apart at the seams. Morale problems, drug problems. No one cared to talk about it. Talk didn't change anything. Protest didn't change anything. Change didn't change anything. There seemed to be an across-the-board surrender to despair. An absentminded despair, not very depressing, almost cheerful. A peculiarly American type of despair, it didn't stop people from having a terrific time on weekends.

Everyone felt powerless. Blacks felt powerless, as did all minorities; middle-class whites felt powerless, corporations felt powerless, unions felt powerless, women felt powerless, environmentalists and consumer groups felt powerless, homosexuals felt powerless and thugs who preyed on homosexuals felt powerless, and the police felt powerless. The rich complained about their powerlessness as, of course, did the poor and the employed and the unemployed.

Powerlessness is my meat, home base, what I like best to draw about. So I did not think Jerry Ford was bland and boring, as other writers and cartoonists did. I loved the difference between his good-guy image and his bad-guy policies. I loved his slowness, his bumbling good nature.

He was the first of our nostalgia presidents, in office not to do good but be good, calm our nerves after the wicked presidencies of Johnson and Nixon, remind us with his wholesome beefy looks of football games and beer blasts and driving downtown on Saturday night in an old Chevy in search of girls in pleated skirts and bobby sox and saddle shoes. Ford was the way we remembered ourselves pre-Vietnam, pre-World War II: Mom's apple pie, the corner drugstore, values mythologized in '40s black-and-white movies, doomed by V-J Day and the Cold War.

He was the embodiment of the void left after the collapse of the American Dream. And he looked the part. He filled space like a vacuum. We focused on his "decency"—what else was there to say? He left Washingtonians tongue-tied, but no matter, the rest of the country was tongue-tied anyway. He was a perfect fit.

I put an empty tin can on his head and drew him as Happy Hooligan, Frederick Opper's foolish hero in the Sunday comics just past the turn of the century. Hooligan couldn't get anything right either, and we loved him for it. I could have just as easily drawn him as Joe Palooka. Another creation he closely resembled was the Frankenstein monster.

HELLO, UNITED STATES GOVERN-MENT. CAN I HELP YOU?

NO, GENERAL MOTORS IS OUT. WILL YOU SPEAK TO ANYONE ELSE?

I'M SORRY. I.T.T. IS BUSY. IS THERE ANYONE ELSE?

NO, EXXON IS AWAY FROM ITS DESK. CAN ANYONE ELSE HELP YOU?

OH DEAR, CHASE MANHATTAN HAS GONE TO LUNCH. I'M TERRIBLY SORRY.

OH, I KNOW! WOULD YOU LIKE TO SPEAK TO THE PRESIDENT?

AND NOW FROM THE OVAL OFFICE OF THE WHITE HOUSE IN WASHINGTON, D.C., THE PRESIDENT OF THE UNITED STATES.

CLUMP CLUMP CLUMP CLUMP

WAIT A MINUTE—

CLUMP

HOW DO I GET THESE DARN SKIS THROUGH THE DOOR?

WAIT! I GOT ONE!

IT'LL BE ANOTHER SECOND OR SO—

NOPE!

THAT'S NOT IT...

OH, DARN!

HEY, IS THIS ON CAMERA?

WELL, WILL YOU DO ME A FAVOR AND BRING OVER THE MICRO-PHONES?

MY FELLOW AMERICANS, THIS IS A GRAVE TIME IN OUR NATION'S HISTORY BUT I WANT TO REASSURE YOU...

I CAN'T BELIEVE IT! HERE I AM, A MERE SECRETARY OF STATE, HAVING DINNER WITH NELSON ROCKEFELLER!

I WILL OBSERVE WHICH FORK HE PICKS UP. I WILL PICK UP THE SAME FORK. BY THIS TACTIC I WILL AVOID A FAUX PAS.

HE IS EATING WITH HIS FINGERS! WHAT SHALL I DO? HE CAN EAT WITH HIS FINGERS BECAUSE HE IS NELSON ROCKEFELLER. BUT I AM A MERE SECRETARY OF STATE.

HE IS WIPING HIS FINGERS ON THE PRESIDENTS SHIRT! THAT MAY BE ETIQUETTE FOR NELSON ROCKEFELLER BUT A DISGRACE FOR A MERE SECRETARY OF STATE!

I AM SICK TO THE HEART! HOW CAN I LOOK THE SECRETARY OF STATE IN THE MIRROR AGAIN WHEN I DO NOT HAVE THE CLOUT TO WIPE MY FINGERS ON THE PRESIDENTS SHIRT?

I WILL GO TO MY OFFICE, BUG SOME PHONES AND OVERTHROW A SMALL LATIN-AMERICAN COUNTRY.

POWERLESS I MAY BE BUT I AM PROUD.

MEMO TO MYSELF RE: EFFECTIVENESS.

CALLED A NEWS CONFERENCE. STATED WE NEEDED TO SEND MILLIONS MORE IN AID TO CAMBODIA TO ASSURE A NEGOTIATED SETTLEMENT.

THEY LAUGHED AT ME.

WENT BEFORE A CONGRESSIONAL COMMITTEE. TESTIFIED WE NEEDED TO SEND MILLIONS MORE IN AID TO SAIGON TO PREVENT A BLOOD BATH.

THEY LAUGHED AT ME.

HELD A DEEP BACKGROUNDER FOR THE MOST INFLUENTIAL AND RELIABLE MEMBERS OF THE WASHINGTON PRESS CORPS. CONFIDED TO THEM THAT THE DOMINO THEORY HAS BEEN REINSTATED.

THEY LAUGHED AT ME.

WENT TO A DINNER PARTY. WAS TERRIBLY WITTY.

NOBODY LAUGHED.

I THINK THERE'S SOMETHING WRONG WITH MY ACT.

BEFORE YOU YOU SEE A PITIFUL, HELPLESS KISSINGER —  A MOURNFUL, DESPONDENT FIGURE ON THE WORLD SCENE.

WHO WOULD HAVE BROUGHT PEACE TO THE MIDDLE EAST HAD EITHER SIDE BELIEVED IN HIS SECRET COMMITMENTS.

AND WHY DID NOT THEY BELIEVE? BECAUSE THEY OBSERVED THE U.S. BUGGING OUT ON KISSINGER IN SOUTH VIETNAM AND CAMBODIA.

AND THEY SAID, "IF THE U.S. CONGRESS AND ITS PEOPLE WILL NOT UNITE BEHIND ITS KISSINGER ON INDO CHINA — HOW CAN WE TRUST THEIR CULPABILITY ON THE MIDDLE EAST?"

AND POOR, MORTIFIED KISSINGER, HAVING NO REPLY, SILENTLY PACKED HIS BAGS AND RETURNED HOME.

I HOPE YOU ISOLATIONISTS ARE SATISFIED!

YOU WISH A JOB AT STATE? LIST YOUR QUALIFICATIONS.

IN 1954 I WARNED AGAINST OUR FINANCING FRENCH COLONIALISM IN INDO-CHINA.

IN 1962 I PREDICTED THAT COMMITTING U.S. ADVISORS TO SOUTH VIETNAM WOULD LEAD TO AN AMERICAN WAR.

IN 1965 I DENOUNCED THE BOMBING OF NORTH VIETNAM AS COUNTER-PRODUCTIVE.

IN 1970 I PROTESTED THAT INVADING CAMBODIA COULD ONLY LEAD TO DISASTER.

I'M SORRY. YOU ARE NOT QUALIFIED FOR THE STATE DEPT.

BUT I'VE BEEN **RIGHT** SINCE 1954!

RIGHT AND WRONG IS FOR HISTORIANS. YOU DO NOT FIT IN WITH THE TEAM.

WHO LOST VIET NAM?

"NOT I," SAID IKE. "I JUST SENT MONEY."

"NOT I" SAID JACK. "I JUST SENT AD-VISORS."

"NOT I," SAID LYNDON. "I JUST FOLLOWED JACK."

"NOT I," SAID DICK. "I JUST HONORED JACK AND LYNDON'S COMMITMENTS."

"NOT I," SAID JERRY. "WHAT WAS THE QUESTION?"

"**YOU** LOST VIET NAM," SAID HENRY, "BECAUSE YOU DIDN'T TRUST YOUR LEADERS."

I HATED THE WAY I TURNED OUT..

SO EVERYTHING MY MOTHER DID WITH ME I HAVE TRIED TO DO THE OPPOSITE WITH MY JENNIFER.

MOTHER WAS POSSESSIVE. I ENCOURAGED INDEPENDENCE.

MOTHER WAS MANIPULATIVE. I HAVE BEEN DIRECT.

MOTHER WAS SECRETIVE. I HAVE BEEN OPEN.

MOTHER WAS EVASIVE. I HAVE BEEN DECISIVE.

NOW MY WORK IS DONE. JENNIFER IS GROWN.

THE EXACT IMAGE OF MOTHER.

THE CRITIC ON THE MORNING PAPER SAID OF MY FIRST PLAY "INEPT." THE CRITIC ON THE AFTERNOON PAPER SAID: "DRIVEL."

BOTH REVIEWS TOTALLY MISUNDERSTOOD THE PLAY.

THE CRITIC ON THE MORNING PAPER SAID OF MY SECOND PLAY: "PRETENTIOUS." THE CRITIC ON THE AFTERNOON PAPER SAID: "ABHORRENT."

BOTH REVIEWS TOTALLY MISUNDERSTOOD THE PLAY.

THE CRITIC ON THE MORNING PAPER SAID OF MY THIRD PLAY: "A SMASH HIT!" THE CRITIC ON THE AFTERNOON PAPER SAID: "A TRIUMPH!"

BOTH REVIEWS TOTALLY MISUNDERSTOOD THE PLAY.

THEY ARE NOW MISUNDERSTANDING TO MY ADVANTAGE.

IN THE ARTS THAT'S KNOWN AS SUCCESS.

I HAD A FIGHT WITH MY BOSS.   I WISHED HIM DEAD.

THREE YEARS LATER—   HE WAS RUN OVER BY A CAR.

BOSS RIP

I HAD A FIGHT WITH MY LANDLORD.   I WISHED HIM DEAD.

FIVE YEARS LATER—   HE DROWNED.

I HAD A FIGHT WITH MY SON.   I WISHED HIM DEAD.

FIFTEEN YEARS LATER—   HE'S SIX FEET TALL AND TWO HUNDRED POUNDS.

I LIVE IN TERROR.

SOMEDAY HE MAY INHERIT MY POWER.

I AM LOVED.

PEOPLE NEED ME, WORSHIP ME, CAN'T LIVE WITHOUT ME—

GO CRAZY WHEN I DON'T COME ACROSS WITH WHAT THEY WANT.

I SHAPE LIVES. I TEACH: HOW TO SHOOT. WHAT TO BUY.

I DRAIN EMPTINESS FROM LIVES. FILL THE VOID WITH JUNK. PEOPLE ARE GRATEFUL.

I AM THE GIVER OF NEWS. OPINIONS DON'T EXIST WITHOUT ME.

I AM THE INSIDES OF YOUR HEAD.

IF YOU WANTED A GROSS NATIONAL PRODUCT, YOU GOT IT.

AS I STOOD HIGH ON A HILL OVERLOOKING THE CITY...

I SPOTTED THE WAVES OF RADIO ACTIVE GAS LEAKING FROM THE NUCLEAR POWER PLANT...

RISING TO MIX WITH THE FUMES OF THE SST AS IT LANDED AT THE AIRPORT...

A SHORT DISTANCE FROM THE CHEMICAL PLANT THAT SPOILED THE RIVER.

AND I WONDERED: IS THERE ANY ANSWER TO CORPORATE GREED?

AND A VOICE FROM A CLOUD ANSWERED: "YES, MY SON!" AND I CRIED: "WHAT? WHAT?"

BUT A HIGH RISE OFFICE BUILDING SHOT UP THROUGH THE CLOUD...

AND A VOICE FROM THE TOWER OF THE OFFICE BUILDING WHISPERED: "A MILLION IN SMALL BILLS AND I'LL TELL YOU."

180

THE CITIES DEFAULT. ESSENTIAL SERVICES BREAK DOWN.

PEOPLE CAN'T GET TO WORK. INDUSTRY EVACUATES.

UNEMPLOYMENT SOARS. CRIME SOARS. THE MIDDLE CLASS EVACUATES.

THE CITIES ARE BLACK, HISPANIC, POVERTY STRICKEN AND SEGREGATED—

FROM SUBURBAN AMERICA WHERE WHITE INDUSTRY PROSPERS IN THE MANUFACTURE OF FENCES AND ARMAMENTS AND SPY PLANES AND ELECTRONIC SENSORS TO STAVE OFF DARK AMERICA.

WHITE FLIGHT.

THE BI-CENTENNIAL DREAM.

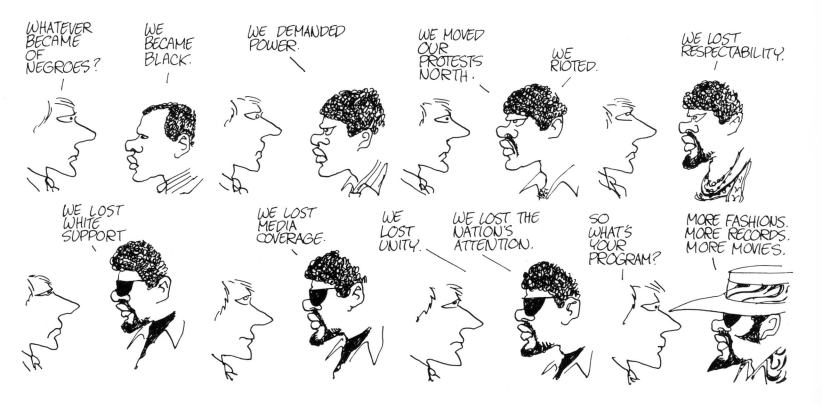

WHATEVER BECAME OF NEGROES?

WE BECAME BLACK.

WE DEMANDED POWER.

WE MOVED OUR PROTESTS NORTH.

WE RIOTED.

WE LOST RESPECTABILITY.

WE LOST WHITE SUPPORT

WE LOST MEDIA COVERAGE.

WE LOST UNITY.

WE LOST THE NATION'S ATTENTION.

SO WHAT'S YOUR PROGRAM?

MORE FASHIONS. MORE RECORDS. MORE MOVIES.

I USED THE FREEDOM OF INFORMATION ACT TO WRITE IN AND GET MY F.B.I. DOSSIER.

IT SAYS: OCT. 12, 1966. PICKED UP GIRL AT CIVIL RIGHTS DEMONSTRATION. STRUCK OUT.

FEB. 3, 1967. PICKED UP GIRL ON PEACE MARCH. . STRUCK OUT.

APRIL 10 1968. PICKED UP GIRL AT McCARTHY RALLY. STRUCK OUT.

NOV. 5, 1972. TRIED TO PICK UP GIRL AT WOMEN'S LIBERATION CONFERENCE. WAS DRIVEN FROM HALL.

YEAR AFTER YEAR OF SEXUAL HUMILIATION AND IT'S ALL IN THE FILES

NO MORE POLITICS.

WORK REMINDS ME OF GIRLS.

LUNCH REMINDS ME OF GIRLS.

MUSIC REMINDS ME OF GIRLS.

BOOZE REMINDS ME OF GIRLS.

MARRIAGE REMINDS ME OF DEATH.

I DON'T KNOW HOW I'M GOING TO WORK THIS OUT.

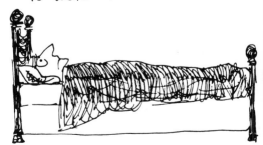

I GREW UP TO
HAVE MY FATHER'S —
LOOKS —

MY FATHER'S —
SPEECH
PATTERNS—

MY FATHER'S —
POSTURE —

MY FATHER'S —
WALK—

MY FATHER'S —
OPINIONS—

AND MY
MOTHER'S —
CONTEMPT
FOR MY
FATHER.

I LIVE INSIDE A SHELL

THAT IS UNDER THE SEA

THAT IS INSIDE A WALL

WHERE I AM SAFE

THAT IS INSIDE A FORT

FROM YOU.

THAT IS INSIDE A TUNNEL

IF YOU REALLY LOVED ME
YOU'D FIND ME.

THE ONE THING I SHOULD HAVE BEEN I'M NOT:

FRED ASTAIRE.

BUT I DON'T HAVE THE TALENT OR DISCIPLINE TO BE FRED ASTAIRE.

SO I DO THE NEXT BEST THING.

I TAP DANCE MY WAY THROUGH LIFE.

I TAP DANCE MY WAY THROUGH RELATIONSHIPS..

AROUND MY FAMILY—

IN AND OUT OF PERSONAL CRISES—

AT TIMES I WISH I COULD SLOW DOWN LONG ENOUGH FOR SOME GINGER ROGERS TO CATCH ME.

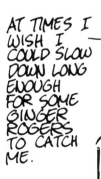

BUT WHEN ONE OF THEM COMES TOO CLOSE I TAP DANCE AWAY.

SENSATIONAL BUT ISOLATED I DANCE ON.

THE CURSE OF FRED ASTAIRE.

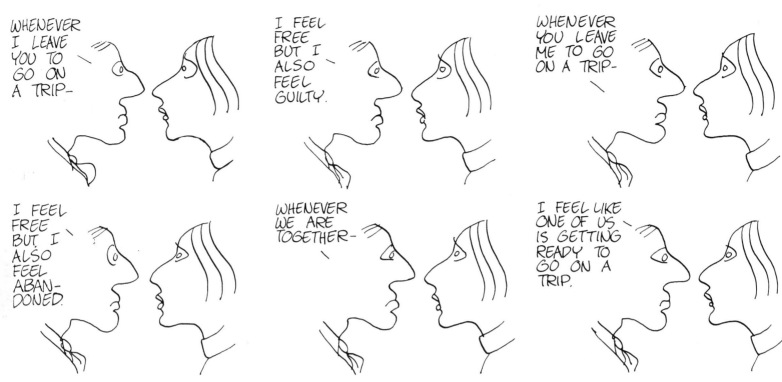

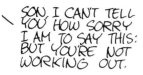 

SON, I CAN'T TELL YOU HOW SORRY I AM TO SAY THIS: BUT YOU'RE NOT WORKING OUT.

IT'S NOT YOUR FAULT. WHEN YOU WERE BORN I THOUGHT YOU WERE THE FINEST SPECIMEN OF CHILD I'D SEEN.

BUT I DON'T FEEL AT HOME WITH YOU.

I CAN'T BE MYSELF WITH YOU.

I HATE SPENDING TIME WITH YOU THAT I COULD SPEND WITH ADULTS I ENJOY.

I'VE LOST 5 OF THE BEST YEARS OF MY LIFE ACTING LIKE A PARENT. IT'S ENOUGH!

SO HERE'S A CHECK FOR $10,000 AND A ONE-WAY TICKET TO MIAMI. GOODBYE, SON —

AVOID MAJOR COMMITMENTS.

I WAKE UP SINGING AND MY WIFE HUGS ME AND KISSES ME AND BEGS ME NEVER TO CHANGE

I SING ON THE BUS TO WORK AND THE PASSENGERS SMILE AND PAT ME ON THE BACK

I SING AT WORK AND THE BOSS HAS TEARS IN HIS EYES AND I GET A PROMOTION

I SING ON THE STREET AND A STRANGER PUTS A DIME IN MY HAND AND ASKS, "HOW IN A WORLD FULL OF MISERY ARE YOU THE ONE MAN WHO'S HAPPY?"

"WHO'S HAPPY?" I REPLY TO THE STRANGER

I SING TO DROWN OUT MY SCREAMING

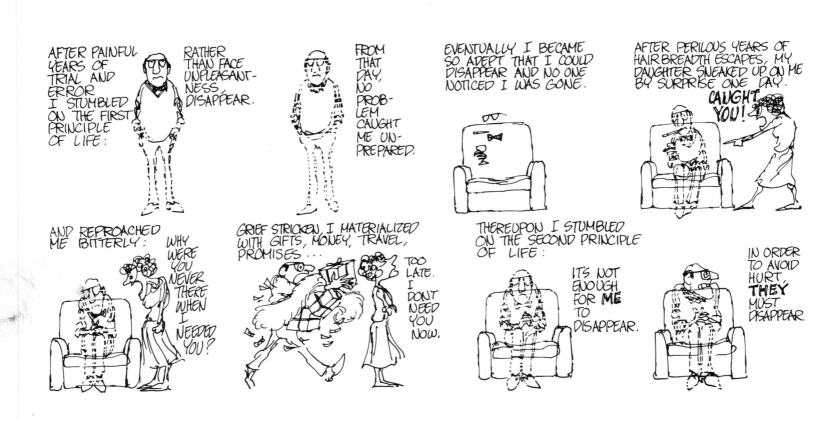

AFTER PAINFUL YEARS OF TRIAL AND ERROR I STUMBLED ON THE FIRST PRINCIPLE OF LIFE:

RATHER THAN FACE UNPLEASANTNESS DISAPPEAR.

FROM THAT DAY, NO PROBLEM CAUGHT ME UNPREPARED.

EVENTUALLY I BECAME SO ADEPT THAT I COULD DISAPPEAR AND NO ONE NOTICED I WAS GONE.

AFTER PERILOUS YEARS OF HAIRBREADTH ESCAPES, MY DAUGHTER SNEAKED UP ON ME BY SURPRISE ONE DAY.

CAUGHT YOU!

AND REPROACHED ME BITTERLY:

WHY WERE YOU NEVER THERE WHEN I NEEDED YOU?

GRIEF STRICKEN, I MATERIALIZED WITH GIFTS, MONEY, TRAVEL, PROMISES...

TOO LATE. I DON'T NEED YOU NOW.

THEREUPON I STUMBLED ON THE SECOND PRINCIPLE OF LIFE:

IT'S NOT ENOUGH FOR **ME** TO DISAPPEAR.

IN ORDER TO AVOID HURT, **THEY** MUST DISAPPEAR.

A DANCE TO SUMMER.

IN THIS DANCE I ASK THE QUESTION:

IS LIFE WORTH DANCING?

AND I COME UP WITH TWO ANSWERS.

YES!

AND

NO.

I AM THUS INSPIRED TO KEEP ON DANCING—

TO PERFECT BOTH ANSWERS.

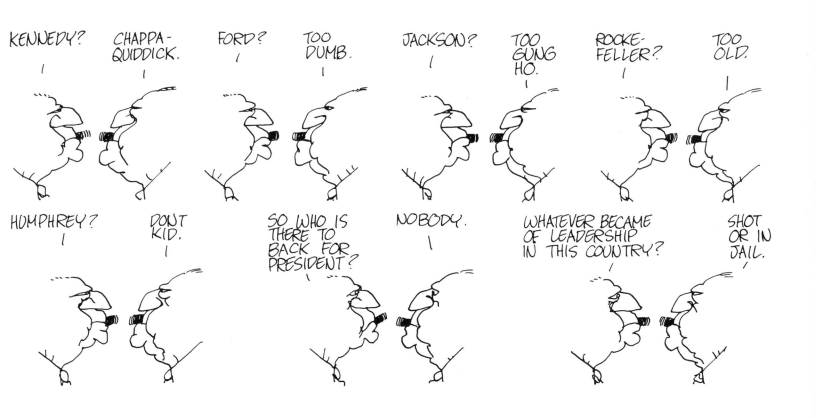

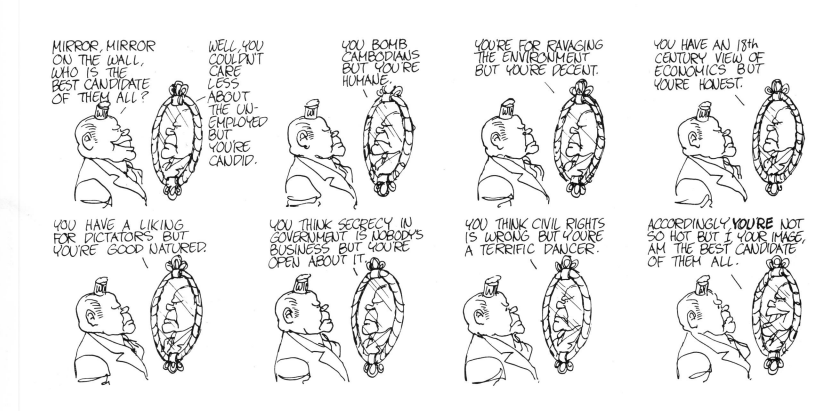

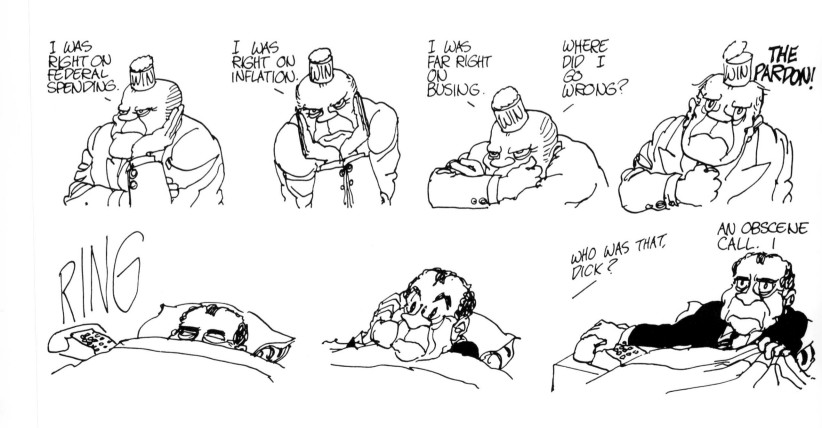

I HAVE TURNED IN MY TIN CAN.

I HAVE TURNED IN MY SPOT WELDED BODY.

I HAVE TURNED IN MY DETENTE T-SHIRT.

I HAVE TURNED IN MY CIA DECENCY MEDAL.

I HAVE TURNED IN MY "STOP FORCED EQUALITY" BUTTON.

I HAVE PLOWED UNDER MY WIN GARDEN.

I AM YOUR LAST FORD CARTOON.

JIMMY THE CLOUD

 The energy level of the country while Jimmy Carter was president was low, virtually unrecordable. Carter had grit, pluck and determination, but he couldn't keep us awake. And he knew it. His obsession with the energy crisis did not have to do with Arab oil but with his personal problems. When Jimmy Carter talked about energy, he meant his own. He could not hold his own attention; he wandered, drifted, his eyes looked sightless, his smile had the vapors. He struggled with the malaise, detailed how hard he worked: hours of reading, awesome study habits, great SAT scores. But he faded before our eyes. He was hell to draw. His image slipped off the page, vanished like the Cheshire Cat.

The real reason the country disliked Carter was not Iran or inflation, but because he was smaller than life. Presidents must, if nothing else, be larger than life. This requires visible energy, energy that resonates, what we have come to call "charisma," by which we mean sexual energy. Carter was the first president since Herbert Hoover with no sexual energy.

FDR was loaded with it: strong, vibrant, handsome and in a wheelchair; *safe* sexual energy, perfect for the prudish '30s.

Harry Truman had abrasive sexual energy. Hardly noticeable at first, it ground away at the body politic like a dentist's drill. "Give 'em hell, Harry!" people cried sadistically; the triumph of small-town, virtuous-aggressive sexual energy.

Eisenhower radiated a warm, solid, husbandly, post-coital glow. Wonder Bread sexuality. He took the Cold War and made it stable, somehow unthreatening. He cared. We cared. You could trust him.

You couldn't trust Kennedy. He introduced dangerous sex to the White House, thrills and chills, fast rides, fast girls, Bay of Pigs, hookers, Mafia, movie stars, missile crisis. He loved us and left us. Our loins ache for him yet.

LBJ: raw, unharnessed cock-thumping-on-the-Oval-Office-desk sexual energy. It was as if Vietnam were a venereal by-product of his sexual drive. The president banged away to keep his dominos up.

Nixon's sexuality was mean and sneaky. A Peeping Tom, dirty thoughts, dirty secrets, invoking Eisenhower's phrase, "I want to make this perfectly clear," while lowering the shades. A pornographer in the White House, crouching in darkened rooms, hungrily watching football players on TV. Hubert Humphrey didn't stand a chance. Mr. Clean versus Dracula.

Ford was beef-on-the-hoof, but an accident, not a president. Still, he had more sexual energy than Jimmy Carter. Carter, an intelligent man, understood his problem. So he did the *Playboy* interview. He planted the lines that won him the presidency. "I've looked on a lot of women with lust. I've committed adultery in my heart many times." The first candidate to falsify sexual content to win high office.

ON RARE OCCASIONS A DAY IS SO BEAUTIFUL

THE SKY IS SO BLUE

THE TREES ARE SO GREEN

THE FIELDS ARE SO GOLDEN

MY CHILDREN ARE SO DEAR

THAT ALL I CAN THINK OF   IS DYING.

JERRY, KID, IT'S THE PRESIDENT. I THOUGHT ID ADVISE YOU ON YOUR RETIREMENT.

FIRST, GO INTO HIDING FOR A YEAR. LOSING IS A CRIME. SHOW CONTRITION.

NEXT, BUILD YOURSELF A POWER BASE IN YOUR OWN HOME. AN IMPOSING DESK. A FACSIMILE PRESIDENTIAL SEAL. MINI-FLAGS OF ALL NATIONS.

ALWAYS LOOK EX-PRESIDENT-IAL. SHAVE 4 TIMES A DAY. WEAR SUITS AND TIES EVERY-WHERE BUT THE GOLF COURSE.

WHEN YOU UNVEIL YOURSELF IN PUBLIC BE SEEN ONLY WITH INDUSTRIAL-ISTS. THEY ADD TO YOUR PRESTIGE.

HOLD ONTO THE TV RIGHTS TO YOUR MEMOIRS. CHARGE FOR ALL INTER-VIEWS. GET YOURSELF A GOOD AGENT.

IN 1978 GO TO CHINA.

AND, JERRY, WHEN YOU COME TO VISIT, COULD YOU BRING ALONG AN 18½ INCH SPOOL OF TAPE I FORGOT IN THE RUSH. LOOK BEHIND THE LINCOLN PORTRAIT.

ORIGINALLY I CAMPAIGNED AGAINST A TAX CUT.

BUT MY EXPERTS ARE FOR IT, SO I'M FOR IT.

I CAMPAIGNED IN FAVOR OF WAGE AND PRICE GUIDELINES.

BUT MY EXPERTS OPPOSE IT, SO I OPPOSE IT.

I CAMPAIGNED AGAINST THE B-1 BOMBER.

BUT MY EXPERTS WANT IT, SO I MAY WANT IT.

IF THESE DECISIONS TURN OUT TO BE WRONG DON'T BLAME ME—

I'M THE PRESIDENT, NOT AN EXPERT.

IT'S NOT AS IF I'M QUALIFIED.

HOW DID YOU GET YOUR JOB IN THE STATE DEPT.?

I WAS WRONG ON VIETNAM.

HOW DID YOU GET YOUR JOB IN THE JUSTICE DEPT.?

I WAS WRONG ON CIVIL RIGHTS.

HOW DID YOU GET YOUR JOB IN H.U.D.?

I WAS WRONG ON THE CITIES.

IF YOU WERE WRONG WHY WERE YOU APPOINTED?

WE ARE MEMBERS OF THE CLUB.

WHAT CLUB?

THE RIGHT CLUB.

MADE UP OF GRADUATES OF THE RIGHT UNIVERSITIES WHO WENT INTO THE RIGHT CORPORATIONS WHO MADE THE RIGHT CONTACTS.

THEN WHY WERE YOU WRONG ON THE ISSUES?

NOT BY ACCIDENT.

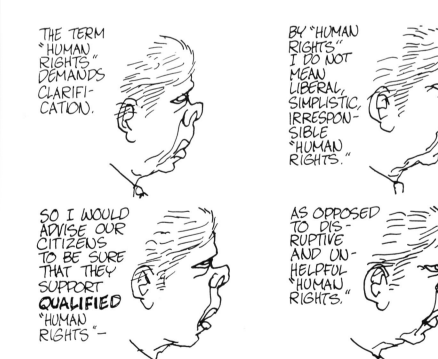

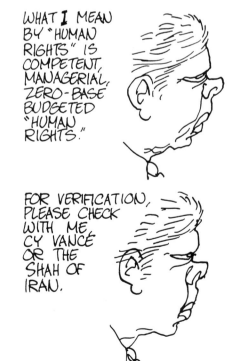

FISH, I AM HUNGRY. — MY FAMILY IS HUNGRY.

THERE ARE FEW OF US AND MANY OF YOU.

I CALL UPON YOU TO DO THE ADEQUATE, COMPETENT AND DECENT THING FOR THE COMMON GOOD.

WHAT ARE YOU DOING, LITTLE JIMMY?

FISHING.

BUT YOU DIDN'T BRING A POLE.

BUT I HAVE FAITH.

THE FISH WILL DO WHAT IS RIGHT.

AND NOW, THE NEWS.

NOTHING HAPPENED TODAY.

NOTHING HAPPENED YESTERDAY.

NOTHING HAS HAPPENED FOR MONTHS NOW.

PRESIDENT NIXON HAS INVADED CAMBODIA... SACKED THE WATERGATE... ERASED THE TAPE... DENIED HE'S A CROOK...

S-SORRY

I DO MISS HIM SO.

SO TENSE MY BODY FEELS — ENCASED IN CONCRETE.

LET ME RUB YOUR NECK.

NOW YOUR BACK.

HIGHER.

GOOD?

LOWER.

FEEL MORE RELAXED?

HIGHER.

EMILY, I'M LEAVING YOU FOR YOUR BEST FRIEND, DOROTHY.

LOWER.

DOES A TREE KNOW I CLIMB IT?

DOES A BROOK KNOW I FORD IT?

DOES THE GRASS KNOW I TRAMP ON IT?

DOES A FLOWER KNOW I SMELL IT?

AM I THE SINGLE UNIFYING LINK BETWEEN THE TREE I CLIMB, THE BROOK I FORD, THE GRASS I TRAMP AND THE FLOWER I SMELL?

THEN I TOO AM OF ECOLOGICAL SIGNIFICANCE.

SAVE ME!

I AM A CRITIC.

I AM NOT A BOOK, ART, THEATRE, FILM, MUSIC OR DANCE CRITIC.

I AM A BERNARD CRITIC.

A RESIDENT CRITIC WORKING INSIDE THE HEAD OF A BERNARD.

HE WAKES UP, I TELL HIM, "YOU'RE LATE." AT THE OFFICE I TELL HIM, "YOU'RE BEHIND." AT DINNER PARTIES I TELL HIM, "YOU'RE BORING."

WHEN HE FALLS IN LOVE I TELL HIM, "YOU'RE NOT GOOD ENOUGH."

ON OCCASION HE CAN'T TAKE ANY MORE REVIEWS AND ORDERS ME OUT OF HIS HEAD.

SO I RIP OFF MY MASK AND SAY, "IS THAT THE WAY TO TALK TO YOUR MOTHER?"

I HATE | THE TELEPHONE. | BECAUSE SHE'S ALWAYS TALKING ON THE TELEPHONE. | AND NOT TO ME. | TO HER THE TELEPHONE IS REAL | AND I'M NOT.

THE TELEPHONE IS HER FRIEND. | AND I'M FURNITURE | THE TELEPHONE IS HER **TRUE** RELATIONSHIP | AND I'M 2ND FIDDLE. | SOMEDAY I WILL MURDER THE TELEPHONE | AND THE WOMAN WILL BE **MINE!**

MEN MAY TREAT US WITH CONDESCENSION...

MEN MAY TREAT US WITH CONTEMPT...

MEN MAY TREAT US WITH BRUTALITY...

MEN MAY ACT AS IF THEY HATE WOMEN.

BUT MEN DO NOT HATE WOMEN.

MEN NEED WOMEN.

MEN HATE NEEDING.

WHAT'S SEX?

IT'S THE THING **THEY** DO TO GET US.

DO WE HAVE TO DO IT?

IF WE GROW UP INTO THE REAL WORLD. IT'S LIKE GOING TO WAR. OR WORK. OR INCOME TAX.

DOES ANYONE LIKE IT?

YOU MAKE YOURSELF. IT'S LIKE PRETENDING TO LIKE ORGANIC VEGETABLES BECAUSE THEY'RE GOOD FOR YOU.

IS IT GOOD FOR YOU?

NO ONE'S SURE. THEY'RE STILL INVESTIGATING.

DOES IT HURT?

I THINK A LOT.

THE WHOLE IDEA MAKES ME SICK.

I THINK IT MAKES EVERYONE SICK.

THEN WHY DO PEOPLE TALK ABOUT IT SO MUCH?

WHY DO PEOPLE SMOKE CIGARETS?

YOU MEAN IT GIVES CANCER TOO?

NO ONE'S SURE. THEY'RE STILL INVESTIGATING.

THINKING
ABOUT
SEX.

THE MORE I
READ ABOUT
IT IN SEX
MAGAZINES
THE LESS
APPEALING
IT IS.

THE MORE I
SEE IT IN
X-RATED
FILMS
THE LESS
EROTIC IT IS.

THE MORE
I LEARN
ABOUT IT
IN SEX
MANUALS
THE
MORE
INTIMI-
DATING
IT IS.

I WISH SCHOOLS
WOULD TEACH
SEX IGNORANCE
COURSES.

THEN I COULD ENJOY IT
LIKE MY FATHER.

DO YOU
THINK I
SHOULD
GO
OUT?

AND
BE
HURT
AGAIN?

MAYBE
THIS
TIME
I WON'T
BE HURT.

THAT'S WHAT
YOU SAID
THE LAST
3 DOZEN
TIMES.

BUT I CAN'T CUT
MYSELF OFF FROM
LIFE ENTIRELY!
MY EMOTIONS
WILL DIE. MY
BRAIN WILL
CORRODE.

NON-
SENSE!
LAUGH.
;CLICK;

HA HA HA
HA HA HA
HA HA HA

CRY.
;CLICK;

BAWWWWW

SEE? YOU LAUGH,
YOU CRY. YOUR
EMOTIONS ARE
IN FINE FETTLE.

AND MY
BRAIN?
WHAT
ABOUT
MY
BRAIN?

I'LL SWITCH
TO THE
EDUCATION
CHANNEL.

NO PERSON HAS
EVER UNDERSTOOD
ME THE WAY
YOU DO.

ENJOY.

IT'S BIG.

BUT IT'S NOT BIG ENOUGH.

IT KILLS MILLIONS.

BUT THEIRS KILLS JUST AS MANY MILLIONS ALMOST AS EFFICIENTLY.

IT'S CUTE.

BUT IT'S **YEARS** OLD AND I'M BORED TO TEARS WITH IT.

IN A TIME OF INFLATION, RECESSION, LOW ENERGY AND MORAL COLLAPSE, LET'S GET BACK TO SOMETHING WE **KNOW:**

AN ARMS RACE.

I DO NOT PANIC IN A CRISIS.

I ISSUE STATEMENTS IN A CRISIS.

I PREACH MORALITY IN A CRISIS.

I HIDE OUT IN CAMP DAVID IN A CRISIS.

I ACT PASSIVE IN A CRISIS.

AND AFTER AWHILE, THE CRISIS GOES AWAY.

OR WOULD YOU PREFER THE BAY OF PIGS, VIETNAM, SANTO DOMINGO AND CHILE?

TAKE BASIC EDUCATION: DRILL, TEST AND BORE THE CHILD.

IT WORKED FOR AWHILE, BUT IT FAILED.

TAKE PROGRESSIVE EDUCATION: MODIFY TEACHING TO FIT THE NEEDS OF THE CHILD.

IT WORKED FOR AWHILE, BUT IT FAILED.

TAKE OPEN CLASS ROOMS: ENCOURAGE NATURAL CURIOUSITY TO MOTIVATE THE CHILD'S LEARNING SKILLS.

IT WORKED FOR AWHILE, BUT IT FAILED.

AFTER AWHILE, ALL EDUCATION FAILS.

KIDS BUILD ANTI-BODIES.

UP AGAINST THE WALL, KID!

I AM THE SUPREME COURT. LET ME ADVISE YOU OF YOUR RIGHTS.

YOU HAVE THE RIGHT TO REMAIN COMPLIANT IN THE COMPANY OF YOUR ELDERS.

YOU HAVE THE RIGHT TO SUPPLY AUTHENTIC-ATED ANSWERS WHEN CALLED UPON IN CLASS.

YOU HAVE THE RIGHT TO BE BEATEN INTO SUBMISSION WHEN REBELLIOUS IN CLASS.

YOU **DO NOT** HAVE THE RIGHT TO KNOW **WHY** YOU ARE BEATEN.

YOU HAVE THE RIGHT TO MAKE ONE PHONE CALL.

THEN I WANT MY OWN PHONE.

TYPICAL!

ME FIRST!

FUN WITH *Language*
WHICH OF THE FOLLOWING PHRASES IS A THREAT TO DOMESTIC TRAN-QUILITY?

1: AFFIRMATIVE ACTION. □

2: REVERSE DISCRIMINATION. □

3: EQUAL OPPORTUNITY. □

4: QUOTAS. □

5: WOMENS' LIBERATION. □

6: DECLINING STANDARDS IN THE WORK PLACE. □

ANSWER: LANGUAGE IS A JOKE. MAKE UP YOUR OWN JOKE LANGUAGE AND TRY IT OUT IN CLASS.

IN BYGONE DAYS AMERICA HAD MORALITY.

FRIENDS OF OUR MORALITY CONTROLLED GOVERNMENTS IN THE FAR EAST, THE MIDDLE EAST, LATIN AMERICA AND AFRICA.

WE SENT OUR FRIENDS MONEY, ARMS, TECHNO-CRATS AND ADVISORS IN COUNTER-INSURGENCY.

AND WITH OUR SUPPORT, THEY DICTATED, KILLED, TORTURED AND PLUNDERED.

UNTIL THEY WERE OVERTHROWN.

TO BE REPLACED BY DICTATORS, KILLERS, TORTURERS AND PLUNDERERS WHO ARE NOT OUR FRIENDS.

THE COLLAPSE OF MORALITY.

THE PEOPLE'S REPUBLIC OF CHINA

INVADES THE DEMOCRATIC REPUBLIC OF VIETNAM

WHICH PREVIOUSLY INVADED AND OVERTHREW DEMOCRATIC KAMPUCHEA.

I AM A MARXIST.

IT LOOKS BAD FOR NOW, BUT WAIT.

HISTORY WILL PROVE THIS NEVER HAPPENED.

CIA IS ILL.

NO COVERT OPERATIONS

CIA IS FEVERISH!

NO POLITICAL ASSASSINATIONS

CIA IS COMATOSE!

NO BREAKINS. NO BLACK BAG JOBS. NO DOMESTIC BUGGING.

CIA IS DYING!

NO MIND CONTROL EXPERIMENT,

COME BACK, CIA! WE'LL GIVE YOU ANYTHING YOU WANT!

IT'S A DEAL.

HE'S WELL! HE'S BACK! HE'S SNEAKY!

HE'S WELL! HE'S BACK! HE'S SNEAKY!

MR. PRESIDENT, WHAT DO YOU SAY TO CRITICISM OF YOUR OIL PRICE DECONTROL PLAN?

A LOT OF BALONEY!

WHAT DO YOU SAY TO CRITICISM OF YOUR WINDFALL PROFITS PLAN?

APPLESAUCE!

WHAT DO YOU SAY TO CRITICISM OF YOUR GAS RATIONING PLAN?

BANANAS!

WHAT DO YOU SAY TO CRITICISM OF YOUR VOLUNTARY WAGE AND PRICE GUIDELINES?

FUDGE!

WHAT DO YOU SAY TO CRITICISM OF YOUR SALT II TREATY?

HORSE RADISH!

WHAT ARE YOU GOING TO SAY TO THE AMERICAN PEOPLE TO JUSTIFY A SECOND TERM IN OFFICE?

CHEESE.

I'M
CONSUMED
BY
NOSTALGIA.

NOT FOR **MY**
CHILDHOOD
BUT FOR
ANDY HARDY'S
CHILDHOOD.

NOT FOR
MY
PAR-
ENTS
BUT
FOR
LEWIS STONE
AND
FAY HOLDEN
AS MY
PARENTS.

NOT FOR
MY OLD
GIRL
FRIENDS
BUT FOR
JUDY GARLAND
AND
ANN RUTHERFORD
AS MY
GIRL FRIENDS.

NOT FOR
THE
BRONX
BUT FOR
#1 SHADY
LANE, JUST
OFF MAIN
STREET,
SMALLVILLE,
U.S.A.

I DON'T
PINE FOR
MY
REAL
PAST.

I PINE FOR
MY MGM
PAST.

MY WIFE
SAID I
WAS
FAT
BECAUSE —
I'M
GREEDY.

SO I
ATE
HER.

MY SON
SAID I
WAS
FAT
OUT OF
INSECURITY.

SO I
ATE
HIM.

MY DOCTOR
SAID I
WAS FAT
BECAUSE I —
DON'T FEEL
LOVED.

SO I
ATE
HIM.

MY MOTHER
SAID
I'VE HAD AN
UNAPPEASABLE
APPETITE
SINCE I WAS
A BABY AND
ONE DAY I'M
GOING TO
EXPLODE
LIKE A
BALLOON.

SO I
ATE
HER

I'M
HUNGRY!

A DANCE TO HOKUM.

IN THIS DANCE I CELEBRATE RONALD HOKUM...

RUNNING FOR PRESIDENT AGAINST JIMMY HOKUM..

ENGAGING IN DEBATES THAT ARE HOKUM...

OVER ISSUES THAT ARE HOKUM...

COVERED BY LOTS OF MEDIA HOKUM.

ON JANUARY 20 ONE OF THESE HOKUMS GOES TO THE WHITE HOUSE AS THE BEST OF ALL POSSIBLE HOKUMS.

AFTER FOUR YEARS WE'LL BE FED UP WITH HIS HOKUM AND VOTE FOR SOME OTHER HOKUM.

HOW COME?

JULY: TO ARMS! TO ARMS! THE RUSSIANS ARE COMING!

AUGUST: TO ARMS! TO ARMS! THE RUSSIANS ARE COMING!

SEPTEMBER: MORE ARMS, MORE ARMS! THE RUSSIANS ARE COMING!

OCTOBER: MORE MISSILES! MORE BOMBS! THE RUSSIANS ARE COMING!

ELECTION EVE: THE RUSSIANS! THE RUSSIANS! THE RUSSIANS ARE COMING!

ELECTION DAY plus 1: WELL, THE RUSSIANS ARE GONE.

HOW COULD THE U.S. TOLERATE SUCH A DRASTIC MILITARY IMBALANCE? IT'S A NATIONAL SCANDAL!

WHEN DID WE FIRST LEARN WE WERE DEFENSELESS AGAINST THE RUSSIANS?

WAS IT IN 1979 WITH BREZHNEV?

EARLIER.

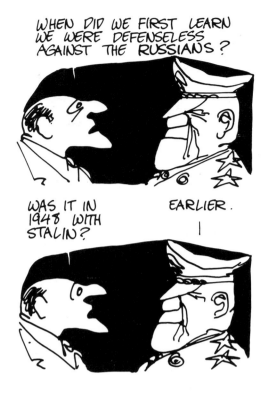

WAS IT IN 1960 WITH KHRUSHCHEV?

EARLIER.

WAS IT IN 1948 WITH STALIN?

EARLIER.

WHEN?

1917 WITH LENIN.

RIDDLE

I AM SMILING.

I AM CRYING.

I AM WEAK.

I AM STRONG.

I AM LIBERAL.

I AM CONSERVATIVE.

I AM LEAVING.

I WAS NEVER HERE.

WHO AM I?

I AM A POLITICAL CARTOONIST'S NIGHTMARE.

SEE THOSE LIGHTS — IN THE DISTANCE?

THEY MAKE ME WANT TO CRY. —

EACH LIGHT IS A HOUSE. EACH HOUSE IS A FAMILY. EACH FAMILY IS HAVING A CHRISTMAS.

THEY'RE EXCHANGING — PRESENTS. THEY'RE SITTING DOWN TO DINNER. THEY'RE SINGING CAROLS.

AND HERE I AM, ALONE.

I'M HERE! WHAT'S THE MATTER WITH ME?

YOU'RE NOT A LIGHT IN THE DISTANCE.

MOVIE AMERICA

Several months into the first year of his presidency, Ronald Reagan went back to Notre Dame. He had never actually gone there; he had gone in a movie, *Knute Rockne, All-American*. Reagan played a football player, Frank Gipp, known as the Gipper, a role made famous not by his performance—few remember it —but by a speech of Pat O'Brien's, the film's star, about the character Ronald Reagan played. This is an early example of Reagan's political savvy and good staff work: He remained off-stage—dead, in fact—while a movie star nominated him into legend.

In his Notre Dame address, President Reagan reminisced about that locker-room speech. Rockne waited years, said Reagan, to make the speech, saving it until he had a quarrelsome, dispirited, and bitterly divided team. To them he called forth the long and tragically departed ghost: "Let's win this one for the Gipper," said Reagan, quoting Rockne. And so that bitterly divided team united as one and wiped out the opposition. History was made. Metaphor was made. At the end of the president's speech, Pat O'Brien was welcomed onstage. The two old comrades, back in South Bend, hugged, tears in their eyes: the Rock and the Gipper.

It was of no concern to the president that *Knute Rockne, All-American* was not a true representation of that time, that game, or that speech. Ronald Reagan was not quoting real facts; he was quoting made-up facts. He was referring to the only history he truly believes in: the movie version.

Months later, the president told a White House audience of Holocaust survivors that he knew for a certainty that the Holocaust was not a Zionist invention, as some right-wing academics had charged. This is how he knew: He was in Europe at the time the death camps were opened, and he saw movies, actual pictures. Ronald Reagan knew about the Holocaust the way he knew about Knute Rockne. History existed only if you visited it in person or caught it on film. Had he not seen timely, on-the-spot photographs, Ronald Reagan might well have spoken of the "Holocaust theory," as dubious of the Holocaust as he is of evolution. No movie was made on the life of Charles Darwin, but if Warner's had, and cast Reagan, you can be sure that today he would believe in evolution.

Ronald Reagan presides over two countries: the United States, about which he is ignorant, and Movie America, about which he is expert. Movie America is a country that operates within the logic, illusion, and structure of a myth. It is a land of small-frame houses on shady-laned streets, dotted with good-natured, plucky, quirky White Protestant families. Individualism thrives. Bureaucracy and handouts are scorned. Large, no-nonsense colored maids occupy all kitchens; big, bluff Irish cops stand on every corner. Movie America has community standards. It has good, safe schools that field strong teams and hold great proms—and on Sunday, the citizens flock out of white picket-fenced houses and parade down tree-lined streets to attend movie-church, where they listen to movie-sermons in which Jesus Christ is the Gipper who died not for our sins but for our gross national product, so that we might go out there and win: a promotion, a ballgame, a boyfriend, a war. In Movie America, one American is worth ten Japs, Germans, you-name-its—and hard times are cheered because every cloud has a silver lining, it's always darkest before the dawn, the moon belongs to everyone, I found my million-dollar baby in a five-and-ten-cent store.

Movie America was born out of the hearts and imaginations of immigrant Jews and first-generation Irish, who as producers, directors, and screenwriters propagated a secular faith, the essence of which was that all Americans could be handsome, charming, rugged go-getters, winners, classless, and white. Movie-faith: the leveling of diversity, the whiting of America. Nostalgia for a time that never existed except on movie and television screens: supply-side fantasies that prepared us for a leader off the studio backlot, well-versed in the dream, waiting in the wings to take over, as the country, demythified and decomposing, with little faith in the future, summoned forth its last hope: the handsome old prince. A hero whose principles were made of popcorn.

In my childhood it was natural in the neighborhood where I lived to prefer movie-reality over real reality—but no one, not even me, wanted to elect it to high office. No one actually believed that the movies could solve our problems. But now we are in a time when we are inclined to think that nothing can solve our problems. The poor will always be with us; blacks and other minorities will always be with us; the old and aging will always be with us. So screw them all.

One of the meanest phrases to come along in our time is: "You can't throw dollars at problems." We threw dollars at the poor, and they didn't go away. We threw dollars at blacks and more dollars at Medicare and Medicaid, and Welfare and abortion clinics. And all we succeeded in doing, if we accept the conventional wisdom, was to get more poor, more angry blacks, more bad health and bad health care, more babies and abortions. This is what is meant when we talk of the failure of liberalism. We mean the failure of hope, of optimism, the breakdown of an ethic made up of idealism and generous impulses, so that today even liberals are quoted as saying, "You can't throw dollars at problems." We forget who first gave us the phrase: Richard Nixon.

But one place remains where it is permissible to throw dollars. You can throw dollars at the military, where we have thrown dollars for years–and yet, according to the Pentagon and its friends, we are now virtually helpless against the Russians. So, throwing dollars at the military is as fruitless as throwing dollars at problems. Our missiles are sickly, our Naval forces are undernourished, our Air Force is on food stamps, our Army, we suspect, can't or won't fight. Clearly, throwing dollars at the military doesn't work any better than throwing them at the poor and the old and the needy and the racially oppressed.

But this is a view with no credibility in Movie America. Living in a time when we believe that nothing can truly get better, that the American pie is shrinking, that the American dream has withered, we lose interest in the rights and welfare of others. When there is no light at the end of the tunnel, only more tunnel at the end of the tunnel, we acquire tunnel vision: us against them, us against our neighbors, my special views, special needs, single interests against yours.

Having turned hopeless, we turn mean and suspicious. When you're suspicious, you see minority muggers under the bed and Russians outside the window–which is why we need more dollars to throw at our police, our CIA, our FBI, our MX and cruise missiles.

Movie America is not, underneath it all, a creation born out of hope; it is a creation born out of disillusion disguised as hope. It is a supply-side nightmare, where we are asked to remember nothing but our fears, nothing but our perceived or misperceived needs. We are to remember nothing that really happened, on which experience can be based. Such memory is to be despised, dismissed as the "Vietnam syndrome" or "the ghost of McCarthyism."

History is nothing more than a series of script revisions. Memory is meaningless, as disposable as diapers. Truth is a matter of trust. Trust in movie faith. Trust in movie ignorance. Trust in a government that sees itself in power primarily to benefit all its friends who earn more than five hundred thousand dollars a year. Trust in a man on a white Cadillac, a man who rides horseback to the depression, a figure of warmth who guts CETA, the ERA, and food stamps, who tries but fails to gut social security and voting rights, a charismatic charmer who believes the budget to be the last ethical principle in America.

I draw Ronald Reagan with mixed feelings. I too grew up in a movie dream, easily preferring the company of Errol Flynn, Cagney, Gable, Bogart, and Astaire to my family, relatives, and neighbors, preferring MGM–

East Side penthouses to the drab Bronx buildings around me, identifying with John Garfield and countless other actors who shook their fists at the Manhattan skyline and cried, "I'll lick you yet!" I too think that the country is not working, that it needs fixing, that it's going down the drain. I too worry about morality and gaze wistfully at those less ambivalent years when America was in black and white, with Mickey Rooney as Andy Hardy and Walt Disney as God.

Ronald Reagan, with his deep-creased handsomeness, stands tall in the White House, John Wayne's answer to our problems. In his wrinkles you can chart the tracks of America's craggy appeal. He is how we might like to picture ourselves if we were packaged for a commercial: easy, manly, courageous, gracious, humble, good-humored, patriotic.

He is the last flickering remains of the American Dream, its embodiment (rags to riches, small-town boy to president), one of the last to believe in its message. But his ease appears foolish; his manliness, too aggressive; his courage, mindless; his grace, clunky; his humility, tasteless under the circumstances; his good humor, a denial of suffering; his patriotism, a threat to us all.

Unlike Jimmy Carter, he is very much larger than life. In fact, he is a movie caricature of ourselves, our values, ambitions, grievances, madness. In cartooning him, I sometimes scare myself; it is like dancing too close to the abyss. I suspect that we will survive him out of dumb luck. And for a while, at least, we will have learned his lesson: nostalgia is dangerous as a philosophy of government; change, whether we like it or not, is out there and must be incorporated into the way we do things; this is not a country of one class or a world of one color, and it is more prudent–even more American–to embrace the fact than to arm against it.

Reagan and his kind, his predecessors and their kind, are not my kind. They are my teachers, however. They teach what not to, where not to, and how not to. They give negative lessons, fine for the uses of satire, which is essentially a negative form. Surviving our leaders is not just a struggle, it is a joy; that is the irony of the work I do. The more outraged I am as a citizen, the more fun I find as a cartoonist. In the long and short run, I may not affect much but the state of my own sanity. The cartoon keeps it in bounds, it continues the illusion of hope, it raises for me the distant possibility of actual solutions to some of our problems. That possibility is my muse. And my rationale. It gets me out of bed in the morning, it makes me read the papers, it forces my mind off unpaid bills and the writing of plays, it humanizes me, it galvanizes me into combat.

See me advance on the White House. See me sit down at my desk. See me pick up my pen. See me attack my enemies: a cartoon of a happy man.

MY FELLOW AUDIENCE... WE ARE ABOUT TO RELEASE **MOVIE-AMERICA.**

AS THE PRODUCER OF **MOVIE-AMERICA,** LET ME LAY OUT THE STORY-LINE.

BOY GETS GIRL. GIRL GETS MARRIAGE AND FAMILY.

FATHER GETS A NEW JOB AND A TAX CUT. MOTHER GETS A DROP IN GROCERY PRICES.

CHILDREN PRAY AND GO TO CHURCH SOCIALS. BUSINESS SKY-ROCKETS.

RUSSIA CAN'T KEEP UP IN THE ARMS RACE AND UNCONDITIONALLY SURRENDERS.

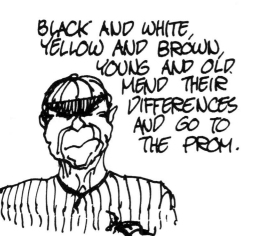

BLACK AND WHITE, YELLOW AND BROWN, YOUNG AND OLD, MEND THEIR DIFFERENCES AND GO TO THE PROM.

WATCH FOR:

COMING SOON TO THE WHITE HOUSE!

ONCE THERE WERE LIBERALS.

LIBERALS TESTIFIED THEY HAD A DREAM OF EQUALITY.

WHITE AMERICA HEARD THE DREAM AND WAS INSPIRED!

LAWS WERE PASSED. BUREAUCRACIES WERE CREATED.

THE BUREAUCRACIES GOT BOGGED DOWN IN POLITICS AND CORRUPTION.

TAXES ROSE. WHITE AMERICA BECAME FACTIOUS AND PARANOID.

CONSERVATIVES TESTIFIED THEY HAD A DREAM OF INEQUALITY.

WHITE AMERICA HEARD THE DREAM AND WAS INSPIRED!

WHITE AMERICA HAS TO DREAM

EVEN IF IT KILLS ME.

WE HIDE THESE TRUTHS TO BE SELF-EVIDENT.

THAT ALL MEN ARE CREATED SERVILE.

THAT THEY ENDOW THEIR JUNTA WITH CERTAIN UNALIENABLE BLIGHTS.

THAT AMONG THESE ARE LIES, ILLITERACY AND THE PURSUIT OF CRAPPINESS.

THAT TO SECURE THESE BLIGHTS, WE NEED AMERICAN AID.

GOLLY! WOW! CAP, GIVE EL PRESIDENTE ANOTHER 80 MILLION!

233

I BELIEVE I HAVE COME UP WITH THE MEANING OF JOHN LENNON'S DEATH.

I BELIEVE THERE IS A GREAT STAR SHOOTER IN HEAVEN WHO PICKS SUPER STARS TO SHOOT.

IF YOU ARE A GOOD LEADER, THE STAR SHOOTER SHOOTS YOU.

IF YOU GET ON THE CHARTS, THE STAR SHOOTER SHOOTS YOU.

IF YOU FIND THE CURE TO CANCER, THE STAR SHOOTER SHOOTS YOU.

SO IF YOU WANT TO STAY ALIVE, DON'T DISTINGUISH YOURSELF.

THE STAR SHOOTER IS WATCHING.

I HAVE HIDDEN POWERS.

NOBODY KNOWS I CAN WILL FLOWERS TO GROW.

I CAN WILL FLOWERS TO DIE.

I CAN MAKE THE RAIN FALL.

I CAN MAKE TREES FALL.

I CAN WILL DEATH TO MY SLEEPING PARENTS BY JUST POINTING A FINGER.

LUCKY FOR THEM I LOVE THEM.

WAIT TILL MY ADOLESCENCE.

YOU BREAK ALL YOUR PROMISES!

YOU INSULT ME IN FRONT OF THE CHILDREN!

YOU CHEAT ON ME!

YOU REFUSE TO TALK ABOUT OUR PROBLEMS!

I'VE HAD IT, BILL!

I'M CALLING THE RELATIONSHIP POLICE!

WE ARE THE RELATIONSHIP POLICE. I'M THE GOOD COP.

I'M THE BAD COP.

WHEN A COUPLE IS IN MARITAL TROUBLE, I COUNSEL THEM.

I THREATEN THEM WITH LONELINESS.

I URGE THEM TO SHARE THEIR FEELINGS.

I BROWBEAT THEM INTO GUILT.

I TRY TO NEGOTIATE A SETTLEMENT.

I BACK THEM INTO A STAND-OFF.

I LEAVE THEM READY FOR A SECOND CHANCE.

I LEAVE THEM NO WAY OUT.

OUR MISSION: TO SAVE MARRIAGE AND THE FAMILY.

IT'S A DIRTY JOB BUT SOMEBODY HAS TO DO IT.

235

"DOCTOR," I SAY, "I AM PREGNANT. I GOT 4 CHILDREN. I CAN'T AFFORD ANOTHER MOUTH TO FEED."

"TOUGH," SAY'S THE DOCTOR. "WE DON'T HAVE A LIBERAL GOVERNMENT ANYMORE, SO YOU HAVE TO HAVE YOUR BABY."

"DOCTOR," SAYS I, "WHAT KIND OF GOVERNMENT IS IT THAT HAS THE RIGHT TO TELL ME THAT I MUST HAVE A BABY?"

"CONSERVATIVE GOVERNMENT," SAYS THE DOCTOR. "THEY ARE CONSERVING ALL THE BABIES."

SO MY BABY WILL BE BORN UNWANTED, UNDERFED, UNEDUCATED AND UNEMPLOYED.

PRAISE THE LORD IT LIVES LONG ENOUGH TO RIOT.

BAN ABORTIONS.

ABORTIONS KILL THE UNBORN.

DON'T BAN HAND GUNS.

HAND GUNS KILL THE POST-BORN.

THE UNBORN ARE INNOCENT AND DESERVE OUR LOVE.

THE POST-BORN ARE GUILTY AND DESERVE WHAT'S COMING TO THEM.

MY SON AND I ARE VERY CLOSE.

HE MAKES ME SICK.

HE SHARES HIS FEELINGS WITH ME.

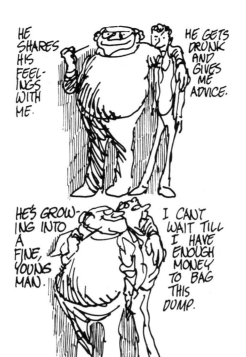

HE GETS DRUNK AND GIVES ME ADVICE.

WE DO THINGS TOGETHER.

IF HE DRAGS ME INTO ANOTHER BOOK STORE, I SWEAR I'LL BURN IT DOWN.

HE LOOKS UP TO ME.

HE CHEATS ON MY MOTHER.

HE'S GROWING INTO A FINE, YOUNG MAN.

I CAN'T WAIT TILL I HAVE ENOUGH MONEY TO BAG THIS DUMP.

DAD, CAN I HAVE — $100 AND THE KEYS TO THE CAR?

ANYTHING, SON!

YOU'RE BORN AND YOU KNOW YOU'RE THE CENTER OF THE UNIVERSE.

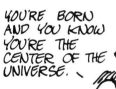

AND CHILDHOOD IS THE PROCESS OF LEARNING YOU'RE NOT THE CENTER OF THE UNIVERSE.

AND ADOLESCENCE IS THE PROCESS OF COMING TO TERMS WITH NOT BEING THE CENTER OF THE UNIVERSE.

AND MATURITY IS THE PROCESS OF FORGETTING YOU EVER THOUGHT YOU WERE THE CENTER OF THE UNIVERSE.

AND OLD AGE IS WATCHING OTHERS BECOME THE CENTER OF THE UNIVERSE.

AND HATING THEM.

MY FELLOW AUDIENCE: WE AMERICANS HAVE LIVED AND PROSPERED UNDER TWO BASIC BELIEFS.

ONE: BELIEF IN THE AMERICAN DREAM. TWO: BELIEF IN THE SOVIET THREAT.

NOW, IN THE SIXTIES WE LOST OUR WILL TO BELIEVE IN THE SOVIET THREAT.

SO IN THE SEVENTIES OUR BELIEF IN THE AMERICAN DREAM FADED AWAY.

WELL, IT'S PLAIN COMMON SENSE, YOU CAN'T HAVE AN AMERICAN DREAM WITHOUT A SOVIET THREAT.

SO AS A STEP TOWARD RESTORING PROSPERITY AND GUMPTION, MY ADMINISTRATION IS REINTRODUCING THE INTERNATIONAL COMMUNIST CONSPIRACY.

SUPPLY-SIDE TERRORISM.

IT'LL MAKE AMERICA GREAT AGAIN.

MY AMERICA IS AN AMERICA OF GUMPTION AN' SELF-HELP AN' SELF-RESPECT AN' NO-NONSENSE.

MY AMERICA IS AN AMERICA OF SMALL TOWNS WITH CORNER DRUG STORES AN' SODA FOUNTAINS WHERE TH' KIDS GO T'HANG OUT AFTER SCHOOL.

MY AMERICA IS AN AMERICA OF MOMS BAKIN' IN TH' KITCHEN AN' DADS WORKIN' IN TH' CORNER GAS STATION OR TH' CORNER SMALL PARTS PLANT OR TH' CORNER FACTORY.

MY AMERICA IS AN AMERICA WHERE WHITE AN' BLACK AN' BROWN FOLKS BURY TH' HATCHETS —

SO'S WE C'N ALL LIVE IN FRAME HOUSES WITH WHITE PICKET FENCES ON SHADY LANED STREETS.

MY AMERICA IS AN AMERICA WHERE TH' CIA AN' FBI BUG AN' SPY ON OTHER AMERICANS —

TO KEEP AMERICA MY AMERICA.

WE HAD A BLACK ON MY HIGH SCHOOL FOOTBALL TEAM.

HE WAS A COMPETITOR. HE PLAYED THE GAME. WE BECAME FRIENDS.

I EVEN TOOK HIM HOME FOR DINNER.

MY BLACK FRIEND DIDN'T ASK FOR AND HE DIDN'T RECEIVE SPECIAL FAVORS.

THE VOTING RIGHTS ACT IS A SPECIAL FAVOR.

NOW SPECIAL FAVORS WEAKEN US. SPECIAL FAVORS WOULD HAVE DIVIDED ME FROM MY BLACK FRIEND.

SO GO-GO-GO-CONGRESS! STRIKE DOWN THE VOTING RIGHTS ACT!

LET'S WIN THIS ONE FOR THE BIGOT.

RONNIE, HERE IS A PROPOSAL FOR AN ALTERNATIVE ENERGY PROGRAM THAT CAN NOT HELP BUT HIT THE GROUND RUNNING.

NUKE-C-COALA!

NUKE-C-COALA CONVERTS NUCLEAR ENERGY INTO COAL INTO WATER INTO A SOFT DRINK.

IT'S A 3 FOR 1 POLLUTANT: AIR, EARTH AND SEA. IT'S WASTEFUL, INEFFICIENT AND COST-EXTRAVAGANT.

IT RAPES OUR NATURAL RESOURCES. IT WILL REQUIRE A TRANSFER OF ALL REMAINING FUNDS FROM FOOD STAMPS AND SOCIAL SECURITY TO FINANCE IT.

AND IT WILL MAKE SIX REPUBLICAN FRIENDS FROM TEXAS, CALIFORNIA AND NEVADA INTO BILLIONAIRES.

MY FELLOW AMERICANS...

IN THIS DANCE I CELEBRATE CONSERVATIVE ANSWERS.

CUTTING TAXES.

CUTTING GOVERNMENT HANDOUTS TO THE POOR AND THE AGED.

BALANCING THE BUDGET.

NOT THROWING DOLLARS AT PROBLEMS.

FREEING THE ECONOMY OF CORPORATE RESTRAINTS.

GETTING GOVERNMENT OFF THE BACKS OF THE PEOPLE.

A DANCE TO SPRING.

BREAD!

A DANCE TO ART.

IN THIS DANCE I ILLUSTRATE PRESIDENT REAGAN'S SUPPORT FOR THE ARTS.

LOVELY, JUST LOVELY.

NOW COME SEE HOW THE TRULY NEEDY DANCE.

INTEREST RATES ARE HIGH.

TAX REVENUES ARE DOWN.

INFLATION IS UP.

BUSINESS IS OFF.

WALL STREET IS NERVOUS.

DEFENSE IS IN TROUBLE.

SO THEY'RE CUTTING DOWN MY SCHOOL LUNCH.

RACIAL INTEGRATION IS ON THE WAY OUT...

BECAUSE SCHOOL BUSING IS ON THE WAY OUT...

BECAUSE PUBLIC EDUCATION IS ON THE WAY OUT...

BECAUSE EDUCATION FOR MINORITIES IS ON THE WAY OUT.

BECAUSE EMPLOYMENT FOR MINORITIES IS ON THE WAY OUT.

BECAUSE WHEN THERE ARE NO JOBS IT'S *DANGEROUS* TO EDUCATE.

OUTLAW SCHOOLS.

WHAT I DON'T KNOW DOESN'T HURT ME.

WHAT I DO KNOW **ALWAYS** HURTS ME.

THE LATEST THING THAT GIVES CANCER... — THE LATEST NUCLEAR SCARE...

THE LATEST ECONOMIC CRISIS... THE LATEST MOVE IN THE ARMS RACE...

THE LATEST POLITICAL ASSASSINATION... THE LATEST SEXUAL BREAKTHROUGH...

NO WONDER READING LEVELS ARE DOWN.

SWIM. SWIM. SWIM. SWIM. SWIM.

TAN. TAN. TAN. TAN. TAN.

PLAY. PLAY. PLAY. PLAY. PLAY.

EAT. EAT. EAT. EAT. EAT.

PARTY. PARTY. PARTY. PARTY. PARTY.

HOME. HOME. HOME. HOME. HOME.

REST. REST. REST. REST. REST.

On Reagan pond

RONNIE, IT'S SO PRETTY HERE ON REAGAN POND.

OH, LISTEN TO THE POOR CHIRP.

HEAR THE DISTANT WAIL OF ROARING BLACKS.

BE MOVED BY THE HUMBLING SOUND OF TIMBER FALLING WHILST MISSILES ROAR O'ERHEAD.

HARK, A JOYOUS CACOPHONY?! WHAT CAN IT BE RONNIE?

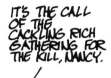

IT'S THE CALL OF THE CACKLING RICH GATHERING FOR THE KILL, NANCY.

'TIS TRANQUIL HERE ON REAGAN POND. PROMISE ME THAT THE BOAT OF STATE WILL SAIL THIS STREAM FOREVER.

'SA PROMISE, NANCY.

NANCY?

MY FELLOW AMERICANS: THIS LITTLE PIGGY WENT TO MARKET.

THIS LITTLE PIGGY STAYED HOME.

THIS LITTLE PIGGY HAD ROAST BEEF.

THIS LITTLE PIGGY HAD NONE.

THIS LITTLE PIGGY CRIED WEE WEE WEE ALL THE WAY HOME.

HA HA HA HA HA HA HA HA HA ONE MORE TIME! WHAT A GREAT COMMUNICATOR.

A TRUE LEADER IS WILLING TO GO AGAINST HIS OWN KIND.

F.D.R. WAS **RICH**. HE DUMPED ON WALL STREET.

IKE WAS A **GENERAL**. HE ATTACKED THE MILITARY-INDUSTRIAL-COMPLEX.

L.B.J. WAS **SOUTHERN**. HE SPONSORED THE VOTING RIGHTS ACT.

I BETCHA THE FIRST **BLACK** PRESIDENT WILL BE AN UNCLE TOM, THE FIRST **WOMAN** PRESIDENT WILL OPPOSE E.R.A.; THE FIRST **JEWISH** PRESIDENT WILL RECOGNIZE THE P.L.O.

I'M THE FIRST **OLD** PRESIDENT.

SOCIAL SECURITY MUST GO.

RECESSION HAS ITS GOOD POINTS.

RECESSION BRINGS DOWN INFLATION.

RECESSION LOWERS INTEREST RATES.

RECESSION WILL MAKE LIFE MORE BEARABLE FOR THE MIDDLE CLASS.

BUT WHAT DO WE DO ABOUT THE OLD, THE POOR AND THE UNEMPLOYED?

THE OLD DIE. THE POOR STARVE. THE UNEMPLOYED GO INTO THE MILITARY.

NOT PERFECT, MAYBE, BUT IT'S A BEGINNING.

When I begin the Begin

So let me begin the Begin — Let me bomb.

Let me bomb bomb bomb bomb bomb in retaliation.

I bring forth the bursts of missiles so splendid.

I bring forth the joy of Israel reveng-ed.

Let me wipe out the P.L.O. to preserve our nation.

I bring forth violence supreme.

A middle east serene — With F-16

When I begin the Begin.

UNCLE MAX SAYS, WHEN ARABS KILL JEWS, THE WORLD FORGIVES; WHEN JEWS KILL ARABS, THE WORLD IS OUTRAGED.

UNCLE JAKE SAYS, IT'S A MORAL DISGRACE THAT MORE IS MADE IN THE MEDIA OVER ISRAEL IN LEBANON THAN THE RUSSIANS IN POLAND OR AFGHANISTAN.

AUNT GUSSIE SAYS, WHERE WAS THE CONSCIENCE OF THE WORLD WHEN THE P.L.O. AND THE SYRIANS WERE DESTROYING THE LEBANESE IN EVEN **GREATER** NUMBERS?

UNCLE IRVING SAYS, OTHER COUNTRIES DON'T GET CONDEMNED FOR DEFENDING **THEIR** BORDERS.

MOMMA SAYS, IN THE END, THE LAST FRIEND ISRAEL COULD LOOK TO IS GONNA BE SOUTH AFRICA.

—UNCLE MAX'S COLITIS HAS RETURNED. ALSO UNCLE JAKE'S ULCER, AUNT GUSSIE'S GASTRITIS, UNCLE IRVING'S GALL-STONES AND MOMMA'S HIGH BLOOD PRESSURE.

—HYPOCRISY IS NOT GOOD FOR THE JEWS.

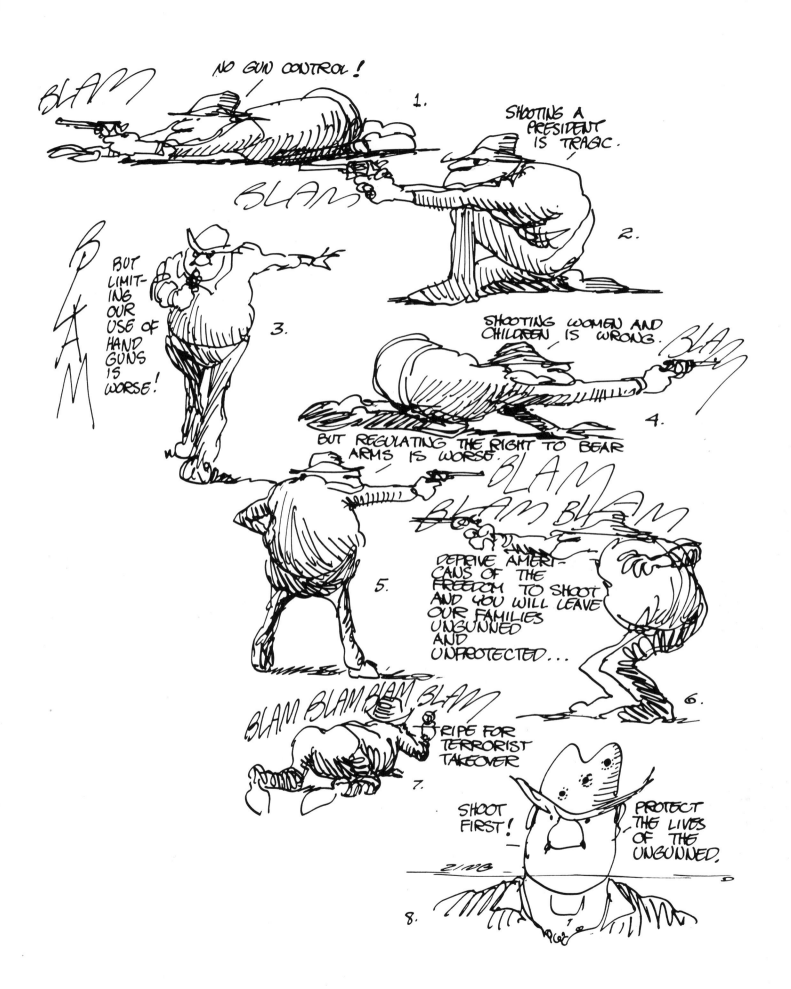

I TRY TO TALK TO YOU ABOUT OUR MARRIAGE. YOU MAKE A JOKE.

I TRY TO TALK TO YOU ABOUT OUR CHILDREN. YOU MAKE A JOKE.

I TRY TO TALK TO YOU ABOUT MY HEALTH. YOU MAKE A JOKE.

I TRY TO TALK TO YOU ABOUT HOW YOU WILL NEVER TALK TO ME. YOU MAKE A JOKE.

5-16

I CAN'T TAKE ANY MORE, NORMAN!

I'M GOING TO KILL MYSELF!

SAY, IS THAT YOUR NOSE OR ARE YOU EATING A BANANA?

I BELIEVE.

I BELIEVE BIG GOVERNMENT IS BAD AND BIG BUSINESS IS GOOD.

I BELIEVE IF YOU LEAVE BIG BUSINESS ALONE, IT WILL COME BACK STRONG.

I BELIEVE BIG PROFITS FOR BIG BUSINESS MEANS PROSPERITY FOR THE LITTLE GUY.

I BELIEVE OUR NATION'S ECONOMIC PROBLEMS WILL BE SOLVED IF YOU JUST BELIEVE ME.

I BELIEVE YOU USED TO BELIEVE ME, BUT NOW YOU DON'T.

I'M GOING TO QUIT THIS PICTURE.

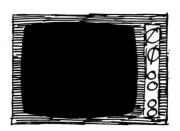

A Note on the Type

The text of this book was composed in a film version of Trump Mediæval. Designed by Professor Georg Trump in the mid-1950s, Trump Mediæval was cut and cast by the C. E. Weber Type Foundry of Stuttgart, West Germany. The roman letter forms are based on classical prototypes, but Professor Trump has imbued them with his own unmistakable style. The italic letter forms, unlike those of so many other type faces, are closely related to their roman counterparts. The result is a truly contemporary type, notable for both its legibility and its versatility.

This book was composed by TypoGraphics Communications, Inc., New York, New York, and printed and bound by The Halliday Lithograph Corporation, West Hanover and Plympton, Massachusetts.

Designed by Steven Heller